The Anatomy of Prayer

THE INTIMACY AND THE WORK

Caleb J. Breedlove

Published by TBG Studio Press, a subsidiary of TBG Holding Co.

ISBN 979-8-9944345-1-2

Second Edition

Contents

I dedicate this book to my mom, Maxine Blackwood-Breedlove. For her constant intercession and faithful example of enjoyable communion with God.

How It All Began

As I was spending time with my family, a question popped up within my heart. The question was, "What must we teach about prayer?" This question stirred deeply within my spirit, and as I sat there, the Holy Spirit directed me to get something to write with. In about 30 minutes, I received from the Lord the outline of this book. With much consideration and prayer, I asked the Lord what He would have do. He replied, "I want you to fast for 21 days; set your heart toward me, and I will give you this book." Thus, on June 12, 2014, I began fasting and praying, asking the Lord to author this book as I wrote it. And so He did.

It was the most supernatural advancement I've ever experienced in my life. It felt as if every morning, I was catching up with the content that the Lord was pouring out into my heart. I felt such urgency within my spirit to continue to write all day, even into the night. I only wrote what I was commanded to write instead of what I "could" write. The content is divided into two main components of prayer: "Intimacy with the Knowledge of God" and "The Work of His Kingdom." I take it not lightly that Lord has entrusted this assignment to me. I am more than honored to have written this book under the authorship of the Holy Spirit and His Word.

This book is dedicated as a resource to further equip the body of Christ with its many insights and also to be in favor of the rising prayer movement that the Lord is leading throughout the world. May the Holy Spirit be with you as you read. My prayer is that you are authentically encouraged, edified, and matured in the knowledge of prayer.

I write only as someone that is available to God, in the name of Jesus, God's resurrected Son, praying continually for the inexhaustible aid of the Holy Spirit. I have not written to criticize or offend, but to share what the Lord has given me to equip the body of Christ. I pray that the Spirit of understanding and revelation will rest on you as you read, in Jesus' Name.

CHAPTER 1

Personal Devotion

What is Prayer?

This question is the foundation of everything written in this book. To us, prayer is the foundation of our relationship with God; thus, we must ask, "What is prayer?" The question of any scriptural practice must be asked of the Holy Spirit and Scripture (see 2 Timothy 3:16-17, John 14:26). The Bible is the thoughtful manual that God has given us, using men as pens to write by the inspiration of His Spirit; thus, according to 1 Corinthians 2:10-14, it is the Spirit of God that reveals the meaning of what is written in Scripture. This is the reason many are confused about what prayer is—because by modeling their own foundation on what they see in others, they have adapted more of a "monkey see, monkey do" tactic, which lacks something that only The Holy Spirit can form in their lives. Paul states the following in his letter to the Romans by the inspiration of the Holy Spirit:

> *Likewise the Spirit also helps in our weaknesses. For we do not know what we should pray for as we ought, but the Spirit Himself makes intercession for us with groanings, which cannot be uttered.* (Romans 8:26 NKJV)

There are a few things I would like us to notice before exploring what Scripture provides about prayer. Firstly, this verse reveals the importance of knowing that we share a weakness within the area of prayer. By stating, "we do not know what we should pray for as we ought," it provides for us the posture of heart we must possess concerning our desperate need for the Holy Spirit. Secondly, before addressing our weakness, it addresses our help. This portion of the verse begins with, "Likewise the Spirit also helps," so I dare to say our weakness will never be the issue in prayer; the deciding factor will always be in whether or not we lay hold of the available aid of the Holy Spirit. The Holy Spirit is here to help! Thank you Lord.

Before continuing, let us pause and pray these simple words: *Holy Spirit, teach and help me to pray. In Jesus's Name, thank You.*

Communion with God

Back to the question: what is prayer? According to the overtones of Scripture, prayer is communion—close interaction—with God. We could go through all of the Greek and Hebrew terms that provide a sense of spirituality to our quest for the answer, but I do not want this study to become more about acquiring knowledge than about receiving revelation for *immediate* personal application. With that said, I want to enter into some discussion of the technical meanings of prayer while trying not to captivate the intellect by displaying words I struggle to pronounce. With all the studies that I have done on this word, "prayer," I conclude to the following statements:

- Prayer shown in Scripture boils down to a simple definition: to ask or call to someone with a need or desire.
- Prayer is generally a vocal practice.
- Prayer is a dialogue, a call and response, a beckoning of one another (generally man to God).
- Prayer is an inward interaction of soul (mind, will and emotions) and spirit, laying hold of the willing human finitude as a sacrifice to the eternal God, to reach an intended state of being.
- Prayer is, at its core, the satisfying of the true internal burning of a flawed humanity to commune with the One and Only Perfect God.

I would encourage you to study the Greek and Hebrew terms with these statements in mind. Now, let us explore some scripture to bring more life to these statements. The book of Psalm, for instance, provides great prayer examples that exemplify the truth in the five statements above:

To You, O Lord, I lift up my soul. O my God, I trust in You, let me not be ashamed; Let not my enemies triumph over me. (Psalm 25:1-2 NKJV)

Cause me to hear Your lovingkindness in the morning, For in You do I trust; cause me to know the way in which I should walk, for I lift up my soul to You. (Psalm 143:8)

These verses show that, though as a king, David faced many battles, he—instead of calling the minister of defense—would go to the tent and call unto the Lord for help. This exemplifies the truth in all of these statements. David's relationship with God through prayer was so strong that David vowed not to rest until He had a resting place on the Earth; in return, the Lord vowed to David that the Messiah would reign on his throne! It was the close interaction in their fellowship—the open communication of prayer—that pulled the heartstrings of God so much that He made a vow unto Himself to honor his relationship with David by establishing his throne forever. Richard Trench, the archbishop of Dublin from 1807-1886 stated: "Prayer is not overcoming God's reluctance, but laying hold of His willingness" (Wiersbe 146).

The beauty of prayer is in God's willingness to respond. Many Christians today desire a relationship without first understanding its intricacies. Hence, prayer has become more of a ritualistic practice than a means of intimacy with the Lord, preventing its true purpose: to draw closer to God. As the Word of God states:

> *And so the Lord says, "These people say they are mine. They honor me with their lips, but their hearts are far from me. And their worship of me is nothing but man-made rules learned by rote. Because of this, I will once again astound these hypocrites with amazing wonders. The wisdom of the wise will pass away, and the intelligence of the intelligent will disappear." (Isaiah 29:13-14 NLT)*

Let us venture into these verses and see how they apply to our prayers—our communion with the Lord. He begins by stating, "These people say they are mine. They honor me with their lips, but their hearts are far from me." Let us narrow it down even further: "These people say they are mine...but their hearts are far from me." This shows that many of us pray without an understanding of how seriously God takes the matter of intimacy; with our mouths we articulate knowledgeable words, yet our hearts are not yearning for communion with the Lord. It is a dangerous thing to lose the flame of intimacy in prayer.

The first thing we must understand is that praying to the Father of Glory is always declaring a profound "I am Yours, and You are mine." If we do not understand this, we are in danger of living in a cycle of deceptive religious activity, believing that our prayers—in and of themselves—are acceptable before God because of our knowledgeable words and not the condition of our hearts toward Him. We will call this the danger zone. Secondly, this same verse ends with a rebuke: "And their worship of me is nothing but man-made rules learned by rote." If or when the conviction of our prayers becomes about following man-made formulas rather than the pursuit of God, we have entered the danger zone.

Prayer is not steps or formulas made by the intelligence of man; prayer is to, in spite of intelligence and human talent, reach for the heart of God and for Him to respond, breaking into our lives to bring forth the intended purpose of unhindered intimacy with Him. This truth is shown in verse 14: "Because of this, I will once again astound these hypocrites with amazing wonders. The wisdom of the wise will pass away, and the intelligence of the intelligent will disappear." In these words, God shows that the best thing to do with children turned "religious activists" is to break in and disrupt their cycle of busy activity so that He can again become the fascination of their hearts, not the subject of their carnal inquiry of knowledge.

Without this understanding, we will not enter into total communion with God. Our experience with prayer will be dry, bleak, stagnant, and ultimately worthless, for prayer without intimacy affects nothing. I encourage you to ask the Lord to ignite the flame of intimacy in your heart again and again!

Encountering His Love

As written previously, God takes prayer—our means of intimacy with Him—very seriously and passionately. But why does the Father of Light busy Himself with weighing the heart of every word that comes from our mouths? The only answer that resounds in my heart is that He does this because He is love. This is shown in a profound statement in 1 John 4:8:

Anyone who does not love does not know God, because God is love.

If prayer is the means of communion with the Lord, and communion is the manner by which we get to know Him, then in prayer we are meeting with God, who is love! His fiery passion to weigh the intent of the heart reveals His zealousness to reveal Himself *as love!* To expound on this truth, here is an analogy:

Say you were the king of a great vast kingdom, where all the people loved you and you fiercely loved them back. Because of this love, you went to battle to protect them; you would walk amongst them and would busy yourself with the small and big affairs of the people, and they pursued you in return. Yet there was this one reoccurring problem; there was something that kept robbing the people of this propelling love: *familiarity.* Soon, the people's love grew cold. They would honor you with their mouths, but within their hearts, they had lost their zeal. Still, they continued praying that you would be involved in their small and big affairs. Thus, as king, you retreated to your throne and stayed there, and anyone who sought you out would abandon their Christmas list of desires for the sake of knowing you, because the fervor of their love had not waned. They found you, and you rejoiced greatly for the purity of their hearts for you.

The king in this situation is God. He searches the earth daily, seeking a heart that has not lost its fervor in love, because that is the only response worthy of His consuming love. God judges the intent of the heart because of His desire to reveal Himself as the blazing love He is.

I have this saying that I think will help you when understanding God being love: *God does not have the capacity not to become what He applies Himself to; this is revealed by Jesus.* (See for example, John 1:1-14, 14:6; 1 Corinthians 1:24; 2 Corinthians 5:15; Colossians 3:11; 1 John 2:2; Revelation 21:6.) The glory of God is that He cannot help who He is. He is blissfully bound by His nature, and He joyfully abides by His character. What a great God He is! The Scriptures further reveal this heart-based nature of His love:

But the Lord said to Samuel, "Do not look on his appearance or on the height of his stature, because I have rejected him. For the Lord sees not as man sees: man looks on the outward appearance, but the Lord looks on the heart." (1 Samuel 16:7)

Every way of a man is right in his own eyes, but the Lord weighs the heart. (Proverbs 21:2)

"I the Lord search the heart and test the mind, to give every man according to his ways, according to the fruit of his deeds." (Jeremiah 17:10)

Let us notice the truths in these Scriptures. The overall point that stares us in the face is that the Lord weighs the heart of all men. Samuel looked at the appearance to judge who was fit to be king, but the Lord's judgments are solely based on the true posture of heart—namely, a posture of heart toward Him, like David, or not.

We have a tendency to become so technical in prayer that we reject the desire of God to reveal Himself to us. This again leads us into the danger zone. The fervor of our prayer—the means of communion with God—depends on our understanding of God's love for us. Many of us know the love of God in a technical way. We know and recite the Romans 8:37-39 promise, that nothing will separate us from the love of God in Christ Jesus, only voicing our knowledge, which, without an encounter, is worthless because of our desperate need of God's love. We even thank Him for His love, yet the words coming from our lips are not alive in our hearts. They can only be made alive through an overflow of love from an encounter with Him. By this means of intimacy in prayer, the Lord's search is not attracted by our intellect's quoting of Scripture but by a yearning within our hearts to experience the truth of Scripture:

> *And we know (understand, recognize, are conscious of, by observation and by experience) and believe (adhere to and put faith in and rely on) the love God cherishes for us. God is love, and he who dwells and continues in love: dwells and continues in God, and God dwells and continues in him.* (1 John 4:16 AMPC)

This verse reveals that abiding with the Lord is a forever-active love encounter. God does not just want to live with us inactively, but Scripture shows that He desires to actively continue with us in love. Prayer is our vehicle to the house of God. When we begin to pray as a means to reach unhindered communion with God, it is for the purpose of encountering Him in the most intimate way that we might know Him! Thus, our personal prayer time with the Lord, when lacking the truth of encountering God's love and responding in love for Him, is more preventive than it is freeing. It prevents us from knowing God and His consuming love.

In a beautiful prayer by Paul, Ephesians 3:14-19 scripts a beautiful imagery concerning the desire for God:

> *For this reason I bow my knees to the Father of our Lord Jesus Christ, from whom the whole family in heaven and earth is named, that He would grant you, according to the riches of His glory, to be strengthened with might through His Spirit in the inner man, that Christ may dwell in your hearts through faith; that you, being rooted and grounded in love, may be able to comprehend with all the saints what is the width and length and depth and height—to know the love of Christ which passes knowledge; that you may be filled with all the fullness of God.* (NKJV)

Let us break this down to better understand this prayer:

1. *For this reason I bow my knees to the Father of our Lord Jesus Christ.*

Paul prefaces this prayer hence: "For this reason I bow my knees..." which shares that the revelation that he is about to share is from a place of prayer. He reveals that it is in this place his petition to the Lord is found and answered. As shown in Romans 8:26, we do not know how we ought to pray, but the Spirit helps us. Then we must believe that this prayer spoken of in Scripture is God-breathed and inspired by the Holy Spirit. Paul says, *"I bow my knees"*: this posture of prayer is what I see to be a place of humility where we cannot depend on human talent or intelligence. But from a position of humble surrender, we can present our Spirit aided prayers to the Lord.

2. *That He would grant you, according to the riches of His glory*

Paul then reveals that through prayer, the riches of the glory of God are available to us. "For this reason I bow my knees, that He (the Lord) may grant you according to the rich treasury of His glory" (Ephesians 3:14 AMP). When you are in the house of God to know Him, He opens His treasury and says whatever you are in need of shall be provided! Like Richard Trench wrote, "Prayer is… laying hold of His willingness" (Wiersbe 146). Everything we receive through prayer—everything, including the power to overcome sin, to healing, to deliverance, even to financial miracles and wisdom, comes from the riches of His glory. Man hides riches in banks and mattresses; God hides riches in mountains and the mouths of fish, for "the earth is the Lord's and the fullness thereof, the world, and they that dwell therein" (Psalm 24:1 ESV).

Daniel says that for God to reveal His glory and sovereignty, Nebuchadnezzar went lived as a wild animal until "[Nebuchadnezzar] knew that the Most High God rules in the kingdom of men, and appoints over it whomever He chooses" (Daniel 5:21 NKJV). God pouring out His glory is not for our namesake but His, as shown in 1 Samuel 12:22, which says, "For the Lord will not forsake His people, for His great name's sake, because it has pleased the Lord to make you His people." It has pleased the Lord to make us His sons and daughters. Thus, He opens the riches of His glory for our benefit and for the glory of His name! Comprehending this, we will always be assured that as we ask according to His will; if so, He will supernaturally fulfill it for His glory. However, in prayer we must not forget that this benefit is a result of knowing Him—the greatest of all riches! The great wealth of His glory to our hearts in prayer must be the glory of His presence. It is the presence of God that makes the difference in our lives.

3. *To be strengthened with might through His Spirit in the inner man.*

Thus, we come to the first of the supernaturally-aided and inspired requests of Paul. His first request to the Lord is to strengthen us with power through the Holy Spirit. The importance of power is great in the life of a believer. Referring to what was written at the beginning of this chapter, we all share in one area of life: weakness.

Notice that Paul did not pray that the Lord give us physical strength, but to give strength to our true selves within. As an exercise, pinch yourself. Go ahead. Now, here is why you did that exercise: it is because I wanted you to know that you are not your body; you live in and animate it. We are a spirit; we possess a soul, and we live in a shell called the body. Let us break it down a little further; we are made in the image of God, and Scripture states that it was when God breathed into man, giving him a spirit, that our bodies were animated as a response to the beginning of our residence within.

As said before, God is spirit, thus we are spirit; yet to connect and enjoy external nature created for us, God made us a body made up of what He had created for us. Furthermore, we possess a soul. I like to refer to the soul as the sovereignty of our spirits. Our souls, which contain our mind, will and emotions are not separate from our spirits, but it is the reason and freewill agent of our spirits. Thus, it is by the reason of our mind (thoughts), our will (inner drive), and emotions (feelings), that we make our decisions and act upon them. Thus, Paul, spiritually aided, asks the Father to strengthen us with mighty power in our inner self, the spirit within the body, through the aid of the Holy Spirit, that we may overcome our weaknesses and have and be what the Lord desires for us! This takes us to our next passage of Scripture:

4. *That Christ may dwell in your hearts through faith.*

The request of Paul for mighty strength through the Holy Spirit is so that Christ may dwell in our hearts through faith. In the Amplified Translation of the same verse, Paul prays, "May Christ through your faith [actually] dwell (settle down, abide, make His permanent home) in your hearts!" (Ephesians 3:17 AMP) Scripture states an amazing mystery that has been given to us as sons and daughters of God. In Colossians 1:26-27, we read this profound statement:

> *The mystery hidden for ages and generations but now revealed to his saints. To them God chose to make known how great among the Gentiles are the riches of the glory of this mystery, which is Christ in you, the hope of glory.*

Christ in me? Yes, and Christ in you! Paul requests that the Father strengthen us with all power that Christ might dwell, reside, and abide actively in our hearts through our faith.

Firstly, on this issue of faith, the request and ultimate goal within this prayer is for Christ to dwell in our hearts, yet the pathway is faith (i.e. *through* faith). In my personal interpretation, Hebrews 11:1 states, "Faith is the bold unwavering confidence that what we hope for will actually manifest" Also, in Jude 1:20 we read, "But you, beloved, building yourselves up on your most holy faith [by] praying in the Holy Spirit" (NKJV). When we pray and lay hold of the powerful aid of the Holy Spirit, we begin building up a pathway of faith—a bold, unwavering confidence of hope within—which allows the revelation of Christ to enter and take residences in our hearts. This is a wonderful assurance that we are not praying in vain without an intended end. But the glorious goal of being strengthened with power and yielding our weaknesses in prayer is so that Christ, His presence, His character, and an unhindered fellowship with Him may be completely operative within us.

Secondly, Christ within us: according to Colossians 1:26-27, this great mystery of glorious power has been made available to us. It shows us that God desires to reveal, not only to us but to the world, His glory and His Son Jesus by coming into our hearts and revealing Himself to us and through us, drawing all men to Himself. This concept was hard for me to understand until I read a sermon by Smith Wigglesworth in which he tells a story of a Russian fellow minister:

A dear young Russian came to England. He did not know the language, but learned it quickly and was very much used and blessed of God; and as the wonderful manifestations of the power of God were seen, they pressed upon him to know the secret of his power, but he felt it was so sacred between him and God he should not tell it, but they pressed him so much he finally said to them: "First God called me, and His presence was so precious, that I said to God at every call I would obey Him, and I yielded, and yielded, and yielded, until I realized that I was simply clothed with another power altogether, and I realized that God took me, tongue, thoughts and everything, and I was not myself but it was Christ working through me." (Madden 60-61)

The young Russian minister explains so simply what we at times struggle to understand. What the Lord desires to do is to clothe us with another power altogether, subduing everything in our lives, to ultimately reside and reveal Himself through our unfeigned intimacy with Him in a mighty way. This is all obtained through prayer with the intention of communing with the Lord to know Him. Now, let us see what the results of Christ coming to dwell in our hearts are:

5. *Being rooted and grounded in love.*

Paul continues his Spirit-aided prayer after asking for power to host Christ inside our hearts. He moves to the crux of it all, saying to God, "God, what I pray you do is to root them and ground them in love!" He is essentially saying, "Deepen their root system in the soil of love." The power of this prayer within our lives is immense!

The reason for the power of the Holy Spirit in this prayer is that our hearts have the strength to be worthy hosts for Christ, and the result of Christ entering our hearts and establishing it to be a fit place to settle down is that we are rooted in love. This goes back to my statement that true personal prayer is an encounter with the love of God. We dumb down the profundity of our encounter with the Lord, cheapening it with the analogy of having a "love affair" with Him. Culturally, having an affair suggests that we are entertaining compromised relationships because the one we have is not enough; in contrast, an encounter with the Lord is worthy of our unreserved fascination and embrace—astounding, awe-striking and altogether beautiful! Thus, Paul prays for us to be rooted and grounded in love.

When you are in that position, you are there to stay. You are not visiting, not passing go and collecting a heavenly reward; you are entering into the field of God and being supernaturally rooted in His love for you and your love for Him!

6. *[That you] may be able to comprehend with all the saints what is the width and length and depth and height— to know the love of Christ which passes knowledge.*

Paul continues by praying that the Father reveals and gives us understanding of the love of Christ, which is shown to be dimensional—having width and length, depth and height. The spiritual rooting and grounding of the saints in the field of God and the soil of His love is what provides the opportunity of growing into the immeasurable love of Christ. To give some application, let us see what Scripture says about these dimensions in other references.

Firstly, to grow in the height of Christ's love is to journey from earthly things to heavenly things. Jesus, the resurrected Lamb of God, called unto John the apostle on the isles of Patmos and John recorded, "After these things I looked, and behold, a door standing open in heaven. And the first voice which I heard was like a trumpet speaking with me, saying, "Come up here, and I will show you things which must take place after this." (Revelation 4:1 NKJV). With all the things that the Lord could have said to describe what was being made available to John He chose to say, "Come up here!" As a result, the Lord began pouring into John and sharing with him heavenly knowledge and secrets. He translated from earthly things to heavenly things and was given access to the unknown mysteries. I believe this also is made available to us according to 1 Corinthians 2:10-12:

> But it was to us that God revealed these things by his Spirit. For his Spirit searches out everything and shows us God's deep secrets. No one can know a person's thoughts except that person's own spirit, and no one can know God's thoughts except God's own Spirit. And we have received God's Spirit (not the world's spirit), so we can know the wonderful things God has freely given us. (NLT)

Secondly, to go higher with and in the revelation-knowledge (experiential knowledge) of the Lord is to go deeper. In this verse, it shows that these secrets of God have been given to us by the Holy Spirit. John the Apostle ventured higher and went deeper into the counsel of the Lord—how high we go is parallel to how deep we go! But it is through prayer that we are given the opportunity. John the Apostle, for example, said these words before he experienced the heights and depths of the Lord: "I was in the Spirit on the Lord's Day, and I heard behind me a loud voice, as of a trumpet" (Revelation 1:10 NKJV).

What activity was John operating in when he was *in* the Spirit? As we read earlier in Jude 1:20, "build up your most holy faith by praying in the Holy Spirit." Thus we know whatever John was doing; it was a form of prayer in the strengthening aid of the Holy Spirit. Some translations assume that John was worshipping in the Spirit, which is a form of prayer. After being in this place with the Holy Spirit, it was then that the heavens were opened to him, and there he experienced the height and depth of the love of Christ. I dare you to read the book of Revelation and see the height and depths of the glory of the love of Christ!

For our last point before the final breakdown of this scripture, we see that in accompaniment with the height and depths of Christ's love towards us is the width and length. Firstly, considering the width, in Isaiah 60:1-5 we read:

> Arise, shine! For your light has come, and the glory of Yahweh has risen on you. For look! darkness shall cover the earth, and thick darkness the peoples, but Yahweh will rise on you, and his glory will appear over you. And nations shall come to your light, and kings to the bright light of your sunrise. Lift up your eyes all around and see! All of them gather; they come to you. Your sons shall come from afar, and your daughters shall be looked after on the hip. Then you shall see and you shall be radiant; and your heart shall tremble and open itself wide. (LEB)

In a prayer meeting, the Lord led me to this verse, and by the direction and help of the Holy Spirit, I began to pray, "Let our hearts tremble and grow wide as you come and take residence within! As we behold your glory, let our hearts tremble with joy and grow wide that the King has come! With all His glory!" Here in this Scripture, the Lord says to His people that His glory will come and permeate us so much that His very light will shine through us, and when we see this, our hearts shall tremble and grow even wider. As I wrote earlier, the glory of the revelation of Jesus will come and reside in us, and as we yield more and more, exchanging our ways with His ways and our thoughts with His thoughts, He will shine greatly through us. I believe and have experienced that the love of Christ widens the heart!

Secondly, let us move on to the next dimension of length. When we think of length, our definition refers to boundaries. Everything has a certain length (i.e. the road is only 3 miles long). When we were away from the Lord we could not and did not enter into His presence because our hearts were not turned toward Him. But as Christ comes and lives in our hearts, the length of how far we enter into the experience of this love is limitless! The Lord tore down the wall that separated us from Him and now invites us to go the length into a marvelous place of intimacy with Him. The love of Christ *surpasses all knowledge*; there is no boundary or limit to His love! He invites us to see how high and how deep His love is for us, how wide and how long His love will take us! We cannot settle for just the knowledge of His love toward and within us, but we must stretch to know by experience the astounding, terrible, and beautifully limitless dimensions of His love. There is always a higher high, a deeper depth, a wider width, and a longer length when it comes to our God; thus we can never lose fascination!

7. *That you may be filled with all the fullness of God.*

Now, we enter into our final point: being filled with the fullness of God. Because the Lord desires to dwell with us, He strengthens us with the power of His Spirit so we can enjoy the fullness of who He is. In perfection, in the Garden of Eden, man had no limit to the knowledge of who God is. It is recorded in Genesis 3:8 that they *heard* the Lord walking in the Garden. They saw the Lord God in all His glory! The fullness of God was available to them! After humanity's first sin, we—through Adam—were cut off from the fullness of God. Thus we began receiving visions, dreams, and visitations; we began building tabernacles and temples and seeing pillars of clouds and of fire. Burning bushes and other supernatural appearances were all we could see of a God who—because of the barriers we established—could no longer reveal Himself in all His fullness. But after Jesus finished the work of the cross, He opened the door wide, that we could experience and be full to the brim with the fullness of God! He ensured this:

> That you may be filled [through all your being] unto all the fullness of God [may have the richest measure of the divine Presence, and become a body wholly filled and flooded with God Himself]! (Ephesians 3:19 AMPC)

Recap

Ultimately, prayer is the means by which we commune with God; it is a response to an amazing encounter with His love. We can only experience the truth of prayer by the powerful aid of the Holy Spirit. As we continue seeking Him, not losing our fervor for His presence in our lives, God, through prayer by the Holy Spirit, gives us access to experience His beauty. The Spirit of Truth unrolls the scrolls of revelation, and we freely venture into it with our hearts!

I encourage you to pray Paul's prayer for the Ephesians for yourself. Here is an example of how you can pray this Scripture: Father, I pray that You would grant me, according to the riches of Your glory, to be strengthened with might through the Holy Spirit in my inner self, that Christ may dwell in my heart through the strengthening of my faith; that I, being rooted and grounded in love, may be able to comprehend with all the saints what is the width and length and depth and height, to know the love of Christ which passes knowledge, that I may be filled with all the fullness of God. In Jesus' Name. thank You!

CHAPTER 2

Our Priestly Privilege

Our Priesthood

To demystify a lot of the concepts of being a priest before God, I want to share with you what it is to be a priest and then enter into the knowledge of how this is parallel with the dealings of prayer. Priests, who are first mentioned in the Old Testament (OT), were chosen people who were responsible for ministering to the Lord. They maintained the order of the house of God and supervised the people's sacrifices to Him, serving as mediators between everyone else and God. Because of their position and purpose, the priests had the uttermost authority to teach the laws of God to others. I like to say it like this: the priests were professionals in private devotion with God. As no one was watching, they ministered and fellowshipped with the glory of God. According to Jewish oral tradition, when the high priest entered the earthly room of God's presence, he was to present the yearly sacrifice of the people for the atonement of their offenses; the high priest would encounter God so closely that he could feel and hear God breathing in and out. What a ministry to have!

Now when we come to the New Testament (NT), the same essential revelation of the priesthood was kept, but the ways changed by transferring the physical to the spiritual. When Christ finished His ministry on earth by sacrificing Himself for our sin, He did away with the physical rituals required by the law God had given to Moses, which the OT priests and Israel had to abide by; in doing so, He became our High Priest.

Before I move further, I would like to unpack these ideas of Christ being our sacrifice and our High Priest: when sin entered the world through Adam (Romans 5:12, 14), its only wages were, and still are, death (Romans 6:23): not only the demise of the physical body, but also the destruction of the spirit, which means total separation from the Lord. Thus, God in His wonderful mercies temporarily set up a system that would serve as a waiver of His judgment on sin and as a prophecy to men of the coming of His Son Jesus. This system can be seen in the OT, where the priests were busy with more ceremonial offerings, included the sacrificing of animals for the sins of the people. According to the Bible, the shedding of blood was necessary:

For the life of the flesh is in the blood, and I have given it for you on the altar to make atonement for your souls, for it is the blood that makes atonement by the life. (Leviticus 17:11)

Because of the way God created life, it is provided by the blood flowing through the veins of every creature, whether man or beast. Without blood, there is death. Thus, because of the consequences of sin, which means a physical and spiritual death for eternity, if you are to continue living after sinning, someone or something must die in your place. In parallel, in the OT, no sinner could enter into the Lord's presence or experience His goodness without first being made holy. God provided a system whereby He in His mercy accepted the lifeblood of innocent and flawless animals as a substitute for the just atonement: the lives of those who had sinned. Therefore, so that God could fellowship with His people, be among them, and reveal Himself to them. So in the OT, instead of men dying instantly because of the consequences of sin, God accepted the innocent blood of animals to be a propitiation for their sins, fulfilling the rightful payment and reconciling his people to Himself, allowing them to enjoy the benefits of His merciful presence amongst them.

When the stage had been set in the eyes of God for the establishing of the New Testament (a New Covenant), He stepped into time with the purpose of fulfilling all the prophecies that had been implied, spoken, and concealed for many ages. In my words, I interpret the words of John as explaining it this way:

So what we knew as only words in the Old Testament was really the reality of God, and God saw fit to take the words He sent to us through Moses, the priests, and the prophets, and fashion the reality of those words into a human, to look and talk like us! We know this because we saw the glory of this reality. He walked amongst us as the Son of God because He was made human, but He was still God Himself, full of that same grace (lovingkindness) and truth that we are acquainted with through the words He sent to us by our forefathers. (John 1:1-14)

Jesus came to waive the consequence of our sins by dying in our place. He was innocent and flawless like those animals in the OT, and by making Himself the sacrifice for our wickedness, He revealed Himself to be very the subject of the revelation that God promised to us in the OT. When He died on the cross, He freed us from physical death—by securing the promise of resurrection to come—and saved us from spiritual death—through the work of the regeneration by the Spirit today—unto eternal fellowship and residence with God.

But how did Christ become our High Priest? First, to define the position, the high priest in the OT was the only person who could come before what was called the Mercy Seat of God or enter the Holy of Holies; this is where God Himself would appear in order to accept or deny the sacrifice given for the people. The high priest was titled this way because he was the only one who had the privilege of access to God Himself. Now when Christ died, the book of Hebrews reveals that He went before the real Mercy Seat of God (the Throne Room of Grace), into the real Holy of Holies and presented His sacrifice for us—Himself—to God as a high priest would. Through this, He became the Ultimate High Priest.

I know that when it comes to deep truths, they can be hard to fathom, but I encourage you not try to understand it within the limited human capacity; when it comes to spiritual matters, we must beckon the Holy Spirit to give us spiritual understanding. Jesus said:

Ask and keep on asking and it will be given to you; seek and keep on seeking and you will find; knock and keep on knocking and the door will be opened to you. (Matthew 7:7 AMP)

Paul, led by the Holy Spirit, encourages us to seek spiritual understanding and revelation, and this only is granted through us giving to God our preconceived and immature concepts, finite limitations and even our ignorance while saying, "Teach me at all costs!"

Pray this with me before you continue: Abba (Father), open my mind to your thoughts and open my heart to your ways. Teach and guide me Holy Spirit through the truths presented in this book. That I may be able to apply it to my life with understanding and wisdom gained through the study of your Word and fellowship with you. In Jesus' name, thank You!

A New and Living Way

I am about to share with you a life changing revelation about prayer. Please bear with me as I explain further what I mean using terms such as the Mercy Seat of God and the Holy of Holies. When you study the Pentateuch (Genesis to Deuteronomy), you will see that the Lord gave specific instructions to Moses for building His house on earth and amongst the people of His heart. I encourage you look at Exodus 26 to see how detailed God was in building His tabernacle; He was very specific about how everything should look, down to how the people should engage with its purpose.

In the innermost part of the tabernacle, there was a place called the Holy of Holies; this is where the Mercy Seat of God was, where the Lord would come and sit to meet with the high priest once a year to either accept or reject the sacrifices for the atonement of the peoples' offenses. Now I want you to know that these sacrifices were not just a matter of law-fulfillment; at this time, God would judge the condition of the people's hearts and decide whether to accept their offering and prosper them for another year, or reject it, withdrawing His presence and blessing.

However, in the New Covenant under the fulfillment of God's ceremonial laws, through Christ, God did away with those imperfect middleman requirements; now, He goes straight to the real purpose of it all: the condition of our hearts. As we read the book of Hebrews, we can see that the earthly tabernacle and temple were somewhat of a replica of what was in Heaven (Hebrews 9). In this way, when Christ died in our place for our offenses, God opened up those true realities for us to enjoy, just as the priests in the OT enjoyed His presence in the earthly tabernacle and temple. In the same book, you will see consistently the phrase: "let us draw near" or simply "draw near" to God, through the sacrifice and position of Christ (Hebrews 4:16, 7:19, 7:25, 10:1, 10:22, 11:6). Of them all, Hebrews 10:19-23 stood out to me:

Therefore, brothers, since we have confidence to enter the holy places by the blood of Jesus, by the new and living way that he opened for us through the curtain, that is, through his flesh, and since we have a great high priest over the house of God, let us draw near with true hearts in full assurance of faith with our hearts sprinkled clean from an evil conscience and our bodies washed with pure water. Let us hold fast the confession of our hope without wavering, for he who promised is faithful.

The writer of Hebrews uses the familiar words "tabernacle" and "temple" of the OT to utter a spiritual matter of the NT. Let us break these verses down:

1. *Therefore, brothers, since we have confidence to enter the holy places by the blood of Jesus*

     First, the writer states we have sure confidence to enter into the holy places. What holy places? If you read the entire book of Hebrews, you will see the writer is referring to the Temple of God in Heaven. This is a very hard concept to explain because it is so spiritual that our finite minds cannot muster the words to express such a deep matter, but through prayer, which is the means of communion with God, we draw near to Him to experience His beauty and the weight of His presence, where we can experience the power, atmosphere and beauty of Heaven manifested in our lives. This scripture shows us that by the sacrifice of Christ, the holy places of Heaven are opened to us, that we might know Him face to face.

2. *By the new and living way that he opened for us through the curtain, that is, through his flesh.*

     To explain this concept presented previously and in this second verse, I must refer to the event of Christ's death that exemplifies this concept of the heavenly holy places being opened for the privilege of those who would draw near to God. In all three of the synoptic gospels (Matthew, Mark and Luke), the same account of an event at Christ's death on the cross is noted; they record that when Christ finally died, the curtains of the temple were torn from top to bottom. What is the significance of this occurrence? It lies in the curtains' purpose, for they hung in the temple at the entranceway into the Holy of Holies, where only the high priest could enter. This was the entrance to go before the manifest presence of God. It was heavily guarded by priests and temple officials to ensure that no one could enter but the high priest, so you might imagine the surprise of the temple officials when they saw it being torn from the top.

     Now, why is this important to know? The tearing of the curtain after Jesus' sacrifice was complete was a physical representation of what happened in the spiritual realm; the true High Priest had entered the real Holy of Holies. Jesus, being that High Priest, opened a new and living way to God through the sacrifice of His flesh, by which we all can come to God. This is not just a physical entrance. If it was, then it would limit how many of us could enter at a time. But this way to the Father, because it is a new and living way, allows anyone who desires to draw near to God to have complete access to His presence in an instant no matter where they are.

3.   Since we have a great high priest over the house of God.

In this statement, we remember that the high priest was the only person who could enter the Holy of Holies, to draw near to God Himself. The high priests of the OT perished because they were prisoners of the Old Covenant and system, but Christ, being our High Priest and the Son of God, was both the founder and establisher of the New Covenant. God established a kingdom upon the revelation of who Jesus is, and its constitution is that all who desire and dare to draw near to God are given access to enter and receive the revelation of who He is. Because the Author and Finisher of our faith, our hope and our freedom, is our High Priest before God, this insures not only our eternal salvation but also our intimacy with God. The greatness of Christ is that He is at all times extending His hands, inviting us to experience the glory of God.

In the OT, the people could only experience the glory of God as servants to Him. As stated in Hebrews 3:5-6, "Now Moses was faithful in all God's house as a servant, to testify to the things that were to be spoken later, but Christ is faithful over God's house as a son." Because of this servanthood, they did not know the father-heart of God, though they were well acquainted with His holiness. This position changes in the NT; Christ being over the house of God as a son means that He completely parallels the desires and father-heart of God as His Son, not just a servant. Therefore, we as sons and daughters of God can draw near to Him through our eldest brother.

4.   Let us draw near with true hearts in full assurance of faith.

In this portion, we are able and invited by the Lord to draw near to Him; the reason for faith is that you might know Him. It says in Hebrews 11:6:

> *Without faith it is impossible to please him, for whoever would draw near to God must believe that he exists and that he rewards those who seek him.*

What an amazing statement. It states that without faith it is impossible to please God; then, it reveals to you what pleases Him, for "whoever would draw near to God must believe!" What an amazing and weighty promise. It goes on to say that when we draw near to God with total assurance that He is real, we must also know with assurance that He rewards those who diligently seek Him. What is the reward? It is not earthly riches or mere temporary satisfaction, but that He takes pleasure in revealing Himself to us! As we pray we increase our intimacy with Him, and He increases His nearness to us. The more you are yielded to the Holy Spirit, the closer you are to Jesus. The closer you are to Jesus, the more unavoidable your nearness to the Father will be.

Pause and pray this prayer: Holy Spirit, take me by the hand, and I ask you to lead me to wherever Jesus is. Show me His face. Father, increase your nearness to me and increase my nearness to you. Open the Heavens wide that I may be filled fully with you, and take pleasure in ruining me for any other satisfaction. Holy Spirit, take me to Jesus. And Jesus, I come to you; take me to the Father.

I encourage you to continue in prayer along these lines before you continue reading. I believe this call and cry to God will open the Heavens wide for you, and God will take pleasure in revealing Himself to you.

5. *With our hearts sprinkled clean from an evil conscience and our bodies washed with pure water.*

Finally, I want to encourage you in this wonderful truth of the glory of personal holiness. Contrary to popular opinion, holiness is not exclusive to outward actions of abstaining from the passions and agenda of the world; holiness is a total separation from the things of this world, an adventure into the things of the heart of God. It means taking pleasure in His pleasure. Holiness is a God-created inner innocence of heart and desire. 1 Peter 1:13-16 shows a picture of this state of being:

> *Therefore, preparing your minds for action and being sober-minded, set your hope fully on the grace that will be brought to you at the revelation of Jesus Christ. As obedient children, do not be conformed to the passions of your former ignorance, but as he who called you is holy, you also be holy in all your conduct, since it is written, "You shall be holy, for I am holy."*

This portion of Scripture shows us that our holiness is not decided by our self-effort. It shows that as we draw closer to the Lord and baptize ourselves in the revelation of who He is, there is a grace in which we set our hope wholly and unchangeably. Our hope is not just in words. Yes, Christ has called you to be holy and totally recreated you for that purpose, and yes, it is only by knowing Him daily and setting your hope on this grace that you are sustained in His holiness.

Holiness is a continual walk of receiving from Jesus, by the help of His Spirit, which is the power to live a life totally consumed with taking pleasure in obeying and pleasing God. Hebrews 10:22 encourages us that as we draw near we have a sure testimony: God has created within us the holiness that we could not and cannot obtain. Our hearts are cleansed of all guilt, shame, and condemnation, and if we used our bodies for sin in the past, it is now totally washed away from us and our record in Heaven.

6. *Let us hold fast the confession of our hope without wavering.*

Have you ever had something so amazing happen to you that you had to voice it over and over again until it became real in your mind? In the case of a man proposing to his girlfriend, the release of nervousness and anxiety within that man's heart when she says "yes" leaves him with an overwhelming feeling of disbelief. Even when putting the ring on her finger, he keeps shouting and laughing with joy: "She said yes! She said yes!" This amazing joy is still less than the wondrous elation of our confession of hope; because Jesus has washed me, I can go freely before the throne of God and delight in the joy of His presence! If you just think about it, it is very hard to get used to that reality. It will take a lifetime, and ultimately an eternity, to fathom the depths of our confession.

I stand in total awe of this: that I have total freedom to access and experience the beauty of the King and Creator of the entire universe who is my Father!

7. For He who promised is faithful.

Even more amazing is that the fulfillment of our confession does not depend on how many times we say it, think it, or even pray it; it hangs solely on the faithfulness of the One who promised us this reality. We all depend on the faithfulness of Christ. In the book of Psalm, there is a consistent theme of trusting in the faithfulness of God. Even more amazing is that His faithfulness is not the result of our actions or belief; it is wholly because He is faithful to His word. The way to consistently see the glory of God is to trust that if He has made a promise to you, He will be faithful to fulfill it! He tells Jeremiah, "You have seen well, for I am ready to perform My word" (Jeremiah 1:12 NKJV). Is it not glorious that no matter what, whether sin, trouble, storm, or even hell and floods, God is still faithful? We can trust that the door of Heaven stands open to us, because He promises that if we draw near, He will faithfully reveal Himself and fill us to the brim!

Recap

Finally, when we pray, vocalizing our desires to God, we are literally transferred from no access to all access to stand before God as His children and priests, and we offer to Him not just our desires or our Christmas list, but thanksgiving and praise because of witnessing His awesome beauty. Let this be your inner vision as you pray: that as His son or daughter, you are literally standing before God, the Creator. This is all attainable because Christ died in our place and reconciled us to God, sitting with Him and standing before Him as our Great High Priest, giving us unlimited access to the Father and allowing us to be completed in His fullness.

Begin to minister to God by singing the songs of your heart as you are drawn closer and closer to Jesus, and just enjoy His presence! *Selah.*

CHAPTER 3

The Preeminence of Christ in Prayer

The Word Made Flesh

I hope you are returning to this book after experiencing God in the preceding section. I pray that every word is a beautiful encounter with the Lord and His faithful love toward you.

In the previous chapter, I shared with you how Christ is our Great High Priest. The greatness of His priesthood and ours as a result is that we can draw near to God and be filled with His fullness as His sons and daughters and not merely as servants. In this chapter, I would like to add another layer to our knowledge of prayer, and that is the preeminence of Christ in prayer. We will explore how Jesus pioneered this experience of prayer in His earthly ministry and how He now sits in majesty holding the integrity of this experience together.

First, I would like to explain what it really means to have preeminence; the Oxford Dictionary explains it as "the fact of surpassing all others; having total superiority." ("Preeminence" def. 1). The Greek definition in the following verse means to be first, or to hold first place. It shows us in this scripture that in all things pertaining to creation and even the New Covenant of our redemption, in all things Christ is preeminent. He was our pioneer into the presence and affirmation of God as a Father. The writer to the Hebrews calls Him our forerunner into the presence of God. He holds the ultimate record. I believe Colossians 1:15-20 may most clearly illustrate idea of Christ's preeminence:

> *He is the image of the invisible God, the firstborn of all creation. For by him all things were created, in heaven and on earth, visible and invisible, whether thrones or dominions or rulers or authorities—all things were created through him and for him. And he is before all things, and in him all things hold together. And he is the head of the body, the church. He is the beginning, the firstborn from the dead, that in everything he might be preeminent. For in him all the fullness of God was pleased to dwell, and through him to reconcile to himself all things whether on earth or in heaven, making peace by the blood of his cross.*

When we read Genesis 1, it says that as the Spirit of God brooded over the water, the first thing that God did was to speak the words, "Let there be light." The misconception is that the first thing God created was light; I propose that the first thing God created was His Word—that through its power, our universe was created and is sustained. John supports this by beginning his account of the gospel with the revelation of the great mystery of Christ being the Verse of the uni*verse*. When God spoke and created "Word," John reveals that He was the Word:

> *In the beginning was the Word, and the Word was with God, and the Word was God. He was in the begin-*
> *ning with God. All things were made through him, and without him was not anything made that was made. In*
> *him was life, and the life was the light of men. The light shines in the darkness, and the darkness has not over-*
> *come it. And the Word became flesh, and dwelt amongst us, and we have seen his glory, glory as the only Son*
> *from the Father, full of grace and truth.* (John 1:1-5, 14)

The writer of Hebrews chimes in on this subject, stating, "By faith we understand that the universe was created by the Word of God, so that what is seen was not made out of things that are visible" (Hebrews 11:3). Similarly, David also shares a key to the mystery when he states in Psalm 119:89: "Forever, O Lord, your Word is firmly fixed in the heavens." To explain how God is the Word, he also states this: "Once God has spoken; twice have I heard this: that power belongs to God" (Psalm 62:11). By these writings, it is evident that these authors knew that all things were made by the power of God's Word.

The fact that the Word had the power to create helps us to understand that during creation, God specifically infused His Word with His Spirit and spoke, and what was in His thoughts was manifested by the administration of His Word. Even before God created Adam and breathed into his nostrils, God was already breathing His Word, infusing the Word with the will, thoughts, character, and life of His heartbeat; thus, Jesus, revealed to be the Word that created all things—was the only begotten of the Father: Christ, the firstborn of all things, made flesh. Nothingness was altered by the power of God's Word, and the Word is Jesus; thus, the originator of the universe was the preeminent and pre-incarnate Christ. Then, after the end of the Old Testament, God saw fit to fashion the preeminent word of His power into a human being, who is the One we experientially know as Jesus, the Lord and Redeemer.

The writer to the Hebrews states that the way to understanding this truth of Christ, the firstborn of creation *as the Word of God*, is by our faith (Hebrews 11:3). Faith is our currency to receive spiritual understanding, and this kind of faith is setting our hope upon the faithfulness of God to reveal Himself to us. These truths require that our minds be thrust into a totally supernatural sphere of thinking to gain spiritual understanding, which we only arrive at by the Spirit of God (1 Corinthians 2:7-12). May this understanding be imparted to us as we fellowship with the Holy Spirit and He opens our hearts, strengthening us to receive the revelation of Christ.

By prayer we are engaging the preeminent One, and as He engages with us, our reward is the increase of our nearness to God. We are in a continual motion of receiving from Jesus by His Spirit in the earth and responding to the Father through Him. Outside of this motion, it is no longer prayer.

There are two major roles Jesus is responsible in the place of prayer, the first of which we will venture deeper into: Christ, the Chief of Intercession.

Chief Intercessor

I have already laid a foundational understanding of Jesus as the Great High Priest, and I encourage you to return as often as needed to refresh yourself with the previous chapter. Our authorization to enter and encounter the realm of the beauty of God is all the result of the two pillars of Christ's priesthood. Building up from that foundation, these coming sections will talk about these two pillars, providing us a proficient awareness of our prayer experience and anchoring our hope and confession of faith, confirming that because of Jesus, communion with God is available to us who believe. In quick summary, the two pillars of Christ's priestly ministry are intercession and advocacy. We will learn that these two are totally different yet inseparable departments of His heavenly pleasure as our High Priest.

Regarding the first pillar, we know Christ as the Chief Intercessor. This is referenced in Hebrews 7:22-25:

> *This makes Jesus the guarantor of a better covenant. The former priests were many in number, because they were prevented by death from continuing in office but he holds his priesthood permanently, because he continues forever. Consequently, he is able to save to the uttermost those who draw near to God through him, since he always lives to make intercession for them.*

We will divide this scripture into 3 specific sections for better comprehension:

1. *This makes Jesus the guarantor of a better covenant.*

Before the writer to the Hebrews made this statement, a foundation was laid about the king-priest order of Christ in heaven. He is both the King of Peace and the Great High Priest over the house of God, just like a certain man in the OT by the name of Melchizedek, who was similarly known to be the king of Salem (which means "peace") and the Great High Priest of the Most High. I encourage you to read the entire chapter of Hebrews 7 to get a better context. Nonetheless, the writer of Hebrews explains that the priests of the OT became priests because of their ancestry. The author further explains that because of this, Jesus, being the High Priest sworn in by God, had to make a greater covenant than that of the old. For if this covenant guarantees that we can draw near to God with confidence, under the stewardship of Jesus, then *because* it would last forever, it had to be more glorious than that of the old covenant. The stewardship of Jesus over the New Covenant guarantees us a more astounding experience with God than that of the Old Covenant.

2. *The former priests were many in number, because they were prevented by death to from continuing in office but he holds his priesthood permanently, because he continues forever.*

The writer continues by noting that the priesthood of the Old Covenant was filled with many individuals because of a simple fact; they were inheriting death because of sin. The apostle Paul reveals in 2 Corinthians 3 that in the former glory (OT), the law of God killed, but now, by the law of the Spirit for those who are a part of the New Covenant, we are guaranteed life. Jesus Himself said that He came and assumed authority in heaven to give us life in abundance (John 10:10). So we must return to Colossians 1:18, which states, "He is the beginning, the firstborn from the dead, that in everything he might be preeminent." Jesus is a greater priest because He was the first to conquer death, which was required by the law of God as the consequence for our sin. Now, He has all authority at the right hand of His Father, as the ultimate One in the systems of earth and in the order of heaven. He holds His priesthood permanently because He lives forever!

3. *Consequently, he is able to save to the uttermost those who draw near to God through him, since he always lives to make intercession for them.*

First, I would like bring your attention to the initial and fundamental word of this verse of Scripture: *consequently*, referring to the *outcome*. The writer of Hebrews uses this word to carry the reader into the *outcome* of this present revelation of Christ. It states that because Christ is the preeminent King and Priest over the House of God, He is able to save to the uttermost those who draw near to God through Him. The word "uttermost" used by the Hebrews writer means "completely and at all times." More clearly, Christ, because of who He is in heaven (Preeminent High Priest over the House of God), is able at all times to provide complete salvation when we draw near to God. This becomes even more defined if we know that the word "save" means, "To heal, deliver, and make whole" or in this context, "To put us in right relationship with God." Thus, because of who He is, Jesus, the One who died and rose again for us, is ready at all times to save those who would desire to draw near to God, to open up the treasury of His presence for healing and deliverance; also, above all other benefits, we can enjoy true intimacy with God. The writer continues with another layer by saying, "[Jesus] always lives to make intercession for [us]," which means that due to Christ's intercessory state of being, He provides and sustains our eternal liberties and heavenly benefits.

To progress farther, we must first know what intercession is and gain the proper insight needed for our awareness to peak and our sensitivity to heighten to this ministry of Christ. The term "intercession" means "to intervene on behalf of another." It comes from the Latin root *intercedere* from *inter-*, "between," and *cedere*, "go," which shows that it is a verb that means "to go between." It is the action of a mediator. In addition, the word "intervene" means "to come between so as to prevent or alter a result or course of events," which includes in a clearer understanding that Christ is always *intervening* for us in heaven, and at the sound of His voice, the heavens bow.

In Scripture, we see that intercession is not only a facet of prayer but is also an issue of position; for example, imagine a weak nation facing war with a great opponent. Because of the disparity in strength, the nation's leaders call for the best negotiator or ambassador; that person becomes an intercessor who represents the whole nation. He or she is given the authority to sit amongst and speak with the leaders of the greater nation with the intent of preventing or altering the projected course of events. Mere lip service or memorized speeches are not effective, because words without the proper access and authority to bring forth change are meaningless to both parties.

Thus, we come to the revelation of Christ as our Chief Intercessor. The writer to the Hebrews already solidifies that He lives in intercession for us, but the question is, why is Christ interceding for us, and who is He negotiating with? Jesus gives great insight into this matter in his words to Peter before He prophesies his three-time denial; He says:

> *Simon, Simon, behold, Satan demanded to have you, that he might sift you like wheat, but I have prayed for you that your faith may not fail. And when you have turned again, strengthen your brothers.* (Luke 22:31-32)

Now, when Jesus begins with saying that "Satan [the enemy] demanded to have you," the word "you" in Greek is plural, so Jesus really said, "the enemy (Satan) has demanded to have you all." Then Jesus followed that statement with, "but I prayed." The word "prayed" is different from the usual Greek word for pray; this one means "to intercede." So more precisely Jesus stated: "Peter, Satan has demanded to have you all, but I have interceded for you."

As we can see in the example above, Christ was interceding for the disciples in the midst of spiritual warfare between the kingdom that He would establish at the cross and the established kingdom of darkness, which shows that intercession is a tool of war. Jesus said, "Peter, Satan has demanded [to have dominion over] you all." Now, why would the enemy demand such a thing? It is because Christ was about to be given over for crucifixion, and for Scripture to be fulfilled (Isaiah 53:3), Satan knew that even His disciples were going to abandon Him, and when this happened, they would be up for grabs in the spirit world. We see this truth in the OT many times over: when the people of Israel abandoned the Lord and His ways, He would declare something like, "Today, you will be given over to your enemies." This happened because when the people abandoned the Lord's ways, they rejected His covenant and His benefit of protection. As a consequence of their abandonment, they were no longer participating in covenant with God; therefore, other kingdoms could claim them.

The same principle of spiritual warfare that was alive in that day is the same as that in Christ's time and even in our present era. We will explain this further in the upcoming chapters. Now that we have finalized why Christ intercedes, our next question is, "Who does Christ address in intercession? Who is he negotiating with?" Logically, it could not be Satan, as God would never stoop to negotiate with a revolted creation. God is unrivaled, His sovereignty and authority demands the obedience of even the evil ones. Yet, Satan has made himself the enemy by struggling against the people and plans of God. Therefore, Christ is not negotiating with the devil; He is negotiating against the plans, systems and lesser powers of our enemy. So, who is Christ negotiating with? It leaves only one other: God Himself.

Be aware that God is *not* against us as the Church. Jesus is not trying to persuade the Father of anything, but He, being one with the Father, knows that all power belongs to God. God is omnipotent, which means He is all-powerful. His power affects *all* things, even nothingness; He spoke the word of His power to "nothing," and it complied willfully with His imagination. Similarly, Christ, being one with the heart and mind of God, knew that in order for us to be protected, He would not have to negotiate with our opponent, but with the One who had created and subdued the enemy. Thus, Christ when he intercedes for us, he bypasses the impotent devil and goes straight to God the Father. Again, understand that this same intimacy is given to us as believers in Christ, and this same ministry of intercession has been given to us as sons and daughters of God.

Before we move on, there is one last part of the verse in Luke 22 that we must notice; Jesus says, "But I have interceded for you, that your faith may not fail. And when you turn again, strengthen your brothers." Here is where our anchor of hope can land. Jesus ensured that salvation would be available for His disciples even in their recovery from the lowest of moments. By this statement, I believe Jesus shows His hope was firmly fixed in the faithfulness of God to answer His prayers, and unwaveringly believed that they would turn to Him again even if they faltered in their walk with Him, hence the statement "*when* you turn again" not "*if* you turn again." We see this reward fulfilled after His resurrection, when the women came to Peter and John and told them that Jesus had risen. When they heard this, they ran to the tomb. Their faith did not fail even in their doubt.

Faith is not the absence of doubts, but the choice to persevere in hope in spite of them. Their triumph over Satan's plan against them was because they were preserved by the intercession of Christ, and at the news of Jesus's resurrection, they turned again to Christ and ran to meet their risen Savior, King, Friend and Brother! This is our hope too! And as we wait on God to intervene and bring forth a change in our days of trouble and need, we can know and have great expectancy, because Christ lives forever, dedicated to intercede on our behalf. In this, we know that God answering our prayers is Christ receiving His glory, and we live by the unfailing reward of Christ's intercession! I encourage you to praise God with me for such a hope and knowing.

Our Great Advocate

Now, let us venture into the insights of the second pillar of Christ's priesthood: advocacy. Not only is it a strong plus, it is also inseparable from intercession. Understanding this will further our hope in Christ and allow us to fall more deeply in love with Him.

According to the Oxford Dictionary, advocacy is the legal authority to be in public support of a particular cause or policy ("Advocacy" def. 2). Under this definition, Christ is the Advocate for those in a relationship with Him, and His advocacy is also closely associated with the advancement of His Kingdom. To provide sufficient knowledge of this, we will explore four areas of the kingdom in direct interrelation with the advocacy of Christ: the Cause, the Council, the Warfare, and the End. This will supply a better understanding of Christ's priestly authority in the realm of kingdom advocacy:

1. The Cause

The key to understanding the heart of Christ's advocacy is in its core; the core purpose of the Kingdom of Christ is that the Gospel of Redemption be preached to all creation. Through Peter's audacious reply to Jesus' "But who do you say that I am?" (Matthew 16:15). We come to know the foundation of the kingdom of Christ's embassy in the earth by the dialogue that Jesus' question begins:

> Simon Peter replied, "You are the Christ, the Son of the living God." And Jesus answered him, "Blessed are you Simon Bar-Jonah! For flesh and blood has not revealed this to you, but my Father who is in heaven. (Matthew 16:16-17)

Jesus declares quite a powerful statement in this moment of revelation; He reveals to His disciples that the revelation of who He is would be the fundamental rock of His embassy in the earth and the cause of His kingdom.

At the beginning of His first mission on earth, Jesus, receiving His affirmation at His water baptism, was thrust into the wilderness by the Holy Spirit to prove His qualifications. Passing the test, He was thrust out of the canal of the wilderness to preach before men with the words of the King: "Repent, for the kingdom of heaven is at hand" (Matthew 4:17). At the completion of His mission, Jesus' mandate to His disciples at His ascension was to go and preach the Gospel of His kingdom and disciple the nations; revealing to them that the mission of his ministry was to introduce the newness of God's kingdom, to author the new covenant, and to establish the ministry of His envoy on the earth, and furthermore, to assume power in all the earth and heaven to make sure that the core cause of His kingdom would be protected and fulfilled.

I am not introducing anything contrary to what is written in the gospels concerning the words and ministry of Jesus; Matthew especially depicts the earthly kingship of Christ; look what He says to Peter next:

> And I tell you, you are Peter, and on this rock I will build my church, and the gates of hell shall not prevail against it. I will give you the keys of the kingdom of heaven, and whatever you bind on earth shall be bound in heaven, and whatever you loose on earth shall be loosed in heaven. (Matthew 16:18-19)

What Jesus was saying is that "I will give you access to heaven and what is declared legal in the heaven, you shall declare legal on earth. And whatever is declared illegal in heaven, you shall declare illegal in the earth." The reason we can do this is because between the two kingdoms (light and darkness, truth and deceit, heaven and hell) we who have joined the side of light are the greater, which is revealed to us in 1 John 4:4, which states:

> Little children, you are from God and have overcome them, for he who is in you is greater than he who is in the world.

With all of that said, here is the revelation: Christ advocates for the cause of His kingdom, and that is the revelation of Himself being revealed to all men. Mentally, this sounds very conceited, but spiritually, it is greatly profound. When Jesus said, "And I, if I be lifted up from the earth, will draw all men unto me" (John 12:32 KJV), what he meant by "lifted up" is not merely songs and worship. He refers to the advancement of the cause of His kingdom reaching all the earth, for the revelation of Jesus is the choice of God to save mankind—the Good News! Paul later adds to this revelation, stating to the Corinthians that the gospel is the power of God to save mankind, which is the reason he decided to know nothing else but the revelation of Jesus and His crucifixion, accompanied and confirmed by demonstrations of the Holy Spirit (1 Corinthians 2). He later tells the Colossians that "in [Christ] all the fullness of God was pleased to dwell" (Colossians 1:19 ESV).

Christ is the number one advocate for the cause of His kingdom. The reason the enemy must flee when we occupy territory is because of the powerful diplomacy of Christ! Again, as Jesus said, what is declared legal in heaven, we will enforce on the earth, and what is declared illegal, we will do the same on the earth. Our declaration as the embassy of Christ in the earth is powerful, especially when we are one with the Word and the will of God. The word "support" in the definition of advocacy means, "To bear all of the weight or give continual assistance to." This means that Christ bears the entire weight of the cause of His kingdom. As Isaiah prophesied, the government of His kingdom is His to carry (Isaiah 9:6).

Jesus is the cause of the Kingdom. David declares in Psalm 110 states that Christ sits at the right hand of God until all of His enemies are subdued under His feet, and the revelation of Christ takes dominion in all the kingdoms of the world. Jesus is the answer to the sin-sick soul of mankind, and Scripture also tells us that God desires all men to know repentance, which is the entranceway to relationship with Him. Thus, Christ is advocating for His embassy in the heavens so that His message of redemption may reach the entire earth. For that reason, the necessary question we must ask is this: how is Christ practicing this advocacy? Hence, we come to the insights of the next dimension of this second priestly pillar: the Council.

2. The Council

Please understand that I write very cautiously and seek only the truth of the Word of God to complete this section; David states a peculiar thing in the Psalms that peaks many bizarre speculations, but I believe it is relevant to briefly consider so that we may receive something of a holistic insight of Christ's advocacy. As stated in Psalm 82:1, "God has taken His place in the divine council; in the midst of the gods he holds judgment" (ESV). Similar passages can be found in Psalm 89:7 and Jeremiah 23:18. Accordingly, the Oxford Dictionary defines a council to be "an advisory, deliberative, or legislative body of people formally constituted and meeting regularly." ("Council" def. 3) Hence, this scripture reveals to us that there is a real court system in heaven and a council that convenes, which the Godhead resides over, and as God, all members are subdued and submitted to obey all of His decrees. Because this scripture also tells us that God takes "His place" in the divine council, we understand that this is what we know in the NT to be the Throne Room of Grace, which Daniel describes in Daniel 7:9-10. The members of this assembly, as far as we know through Scripture, include God, the 24 elders (Revelations 4:4), the heavenly hosts (Job 1:6), the cloud of witnesses (Hebrews 12:1), and Satan (Job 1:6, Zechariah 3:1). The heavenly court operates under the sovereignty of God and His cause; we see a preview of this in 1 Kings 22:19-23, where the council deliberates what to do concerning the kingdom of Ahab, and God's sovereign decree of action was made as a result of the discussion. The writer of Hebrews writes about Christ being our forerunner in the presence of God (Hebrews 6:20). As a result, we can go into the Throne Room of Grace boldly; because of our position with Christ, we are a part of the divine council as well—Christ being our commander and chief, standing on the behalf of His kingdom. Hence, we come to the answer of our question; Christ's advocacy is operative within the divine council of heaven.

An example of how the council may operate today would be this: we, the embassy of Christ's kingdom (the Church), cannot infiltrate Iraq to preach the gospel due to demonic powers harshly hindering us. Therefore, we begin to pray, asking God for access, and for that reason, our prayers invoke the assembly of the divine council. Christ as King of His cause stands to advocate in the heavenly court on our behalf as we also intercede (which we will venture into in the coming chapters), though Satan rages against it. We recognize by the Holy Spirit that the council rules in the favor of our authority to possess Iraq for the Gospel, because Christ obtained legal rights to be lifted in Iraq. Then, we pursue Iraq for the glory of Christ, declaring to demonic authorities and the rulers of the age that their powers over the nation are evicted (Matthew 16:18-19).

Having an open door to spread the message of Christ with the demonstration of the Holy Spirit and with power, casting out devils, healing the sick, raising the dead, and accomplishing great exploits—we, by the advocacy of Christ, progress with the Gospel of His love. This is a great example of what Scripture shows us about the heavenly council, the sovereignty of God, and the greatness of Christ on our behalf in the earth.

3. The Warfare (The Accuser of the Brethren)

Now, we come to our next realm of Christ advocacy: the waging of war against the evil one. Scripture reveals in Zechariah 3:1-2, "Then He showed me Joshua the high priest standing before the angel of the Lord, and Satan at his right hand to accuse him. And the Lord said to Satan, "The Lord rebuke you, O Satan! The Lord who has chosen Jerusalem rebuke you!" What is revealed in these verses may be in the midst of a heavenly council session, where the judgments about the High Priest Joshua were on trial.

When judgments are being sent forth, our enemy the devil is there to accuse the one on trial. Even his known name, Satan, means "the accuser" or "the adversary." This heavenly court preview shows us that the spiritual system of deciding judgments is not solidified unless through warfare. When Jesus was tempted, the devil came to entice Christ to bow and worship him, and in return, Jesus would inherit the kingdoms of the world under his dominion (Matthew 4:8-9). We understand that the enemy is the false god of the kingdoms of the world (2 Corinthians 4:4). His purpose is to hinder the embassy of Christ's kingdom and to have us in his possession as the moment of his eternal demise in hell approaches. He does not want men to experience or even enter into a relationship with God. The enemy is consistently trying to deceive us and claim us for hell because it means one less person will enjoy the splendors of heaven, and one more person will join him in his binding suffering for all eternity. As we see in those verses from Zechariah, he comes to accuse us of our filth and unworthiness to enter into the reward of righteousness.

Ultimately, we come to our revelation of Christ's advocacy in this dimension. Christ, our Great Advocate, is the One who rebukes the devil. Oxford Dictionary explains the word "rebuke" comes from a Middle English that means, "to force back or repress" ("rebuke" def. 4). The Hebrew term *ga'ar* used in this scripture means "to restrain and deter" (Strong's Hebrew Lexicon). After the rebuke of Satan, Zechariah 3:3-5 shows us that all of Joshua's (the high priest) unworthiness was cleansed, and he was clothed in the fine linen of God's righteousness.

John shares from his visions in Revelation 12:10, stating:

> *And I heard a loud voice in heaven, saying, "Now the salvation and the power and the kingdom of our God and the authority of His Christ have come, for the accuser of our brothers has been thrown down, who accuses them day and night before our God."*

This Scripture reveals to us, first, that salvation, power and the kingdom belongs to God under the authority of Christ. Secondly, the demise of that conniving devil is scheduled to be thrown down, and that he is at work even now (because the "throw-down" is to come), accusing the children of God day and night before the Father. However, we have a blessed hope—that Christ our Advocate is appealing for us in the courtroom of heaven! As 1 John 2:1 states, "My little children, I am writing these things to you so that you may not sin. But if anyone does sin, we have an advocate with the Father, Jesus Christ the righteous."

The apostle John, by the Holy Spirit, understood that even in our unworthiness and sin, though we have an accuser day and night before God, we have an advocate in Jesus Christ, who is not just before God, appealing for us, but He has also sat down at the right hand of His Father, making available righteousness by faith in Him intact and fully protected from the works of evil one! Christ, our great Advocate, has already conquered our enemy, and He lives forever as our diplomat in heaven.

4. *The End (The Last Days and His Coming)*

Lastly, we know by Scripture that eternity hangs on two prongs: the first coming of Christ, which has been completed, and His second coming, which we anticipate and prepare for. Scripture states that after the fullness of time had come, Jesus, coming first as Savior and Reconciler, began His mission, which was finished on the cross; it also tells us that we are living in the last days of earth and time, because He will come again soon to subdue the earth and dispel all unrighteousness. In Matthew 24, Jesus gives clear indications of His second coming, yet we do not know the exact day, hour or time of His coming. Still, we have this blessed promise; Jesus states, amongst other indicators of His coming, "this gospel of the kingdom will be proclaimed throughout the whole world as a testimony to all nations, and then the end will come" (Matthew 24:14).

We have a great and hope-filled promise that the testimony and revelation of Jesus as King, Savior, and Lord (which is the Gospel of the Kingdom) will reach throughout all the earth before the true end does come. I encourage you to read Matthew 24 and even the book of Revelations, accompanied with the presence and insight of the Holy Spirit, to get a better understanding of the end times. But let us not get so caught up in the details that we forget the cause of the Kingdom of God and our privilege and responsibility under the authority of Christ to pursue the nations with the Gospel under the demonstration and power of the Holy Spirit.

Finally, Christ's advocacy is heavily related to the events of the end. We are preparing for the coming of the King of Kings, the Lord of Glory, the Lion of Judah! We can rest in the assurance of His advocacy on our behalf—an authority that powerfully clears the way as we spread the Gospel in all the earth, and, as His Bride, join in with His Spirit, crying, "Come, Lord Jesus, Even so come!"

Recap

Two pillars hold up Christ's priesthood: His intercession for the saints and His advocacy. Through exploring those pillars, we have seen that He is absolutely preeminent over all things and is glorious in power and authority. As we have come to know, we can trust in Him as the Chief Intercessor and enjoy daily the benefits of His intercession for us, which includes intimacy with our God, fresh faith even in our doubts, and protection from the evil one. We understand that Jesus is our Great Advocate, safeguarding the success of the kingdom's cause in the Heavenly Council against the accusations of the devil in preparation for His coming to reign on the earth.

I pray that your faith be strengthened and fortified, that you may be immovable because of the knowledge of Christ presented to you in this chapter and by the witness of the Holy Spirit. I encourage you to be activated by this knowledge and to take some time to wait and call on the Lord, for He has given you daily access through Christ to encounter His beauty, hear His counsel, and experience the weight of His loving presence! In Jesus Name.

CHAPTER 4

Yoked With Christ

Come To Me

Beloved, we continue our journey. In the upcoming chapters, we will cover the last of our foundational insights within this book to increase our effectiveness in prayer and assure that the postures of our hearts are one with the knowledge of Christ. Then, we will undertake various facets of our involvement in prayer. But before we move on, I would like you to put the book down and ask the Spirit of Christ to increase His nearness to you. Continue to call upon Him from your heart until you know His presence has filled your location. Stay there as long as you must, and minister to Him as long as you feel you need to. I hope you are returning to this book as His presence is there with you.

I will begin with an experience; during December of 2013, the Lord gave me clear instructions to read the Gospels, amongst other books, for the next two years. As I began reading and digesting the Word, I never felt the need to give myself a time restriction for when I was to finish each book to get to the others. I perceived the need to take my time meditating on every section I read, not rushing the process of "immediate obedience." When I read Matthew 11, the Holy Spirit illuminated many things, but it seemed like as I read from verse 25-30, the words were being burned into my heart:

> *At that time Jesus declared, "I thank you Father, Lord of heaven and earth, that you have hidden these things from the wise and understanding and revealed them to little children; yes, Father, for such was your gracious will. All things have been handed over to me by the Father, and no one knows the Son except the Father, and no one knows the Father except the Son and anyone whom the Son chooses to reveal him. Come to me, all who labor and are heavy laden, and I will give you rest. Take my yoke upon you and learn from me, for I am gentle and lowly in heart, and you will find rest for your souls. For my yoke is easy, and my burden is light."*

I camped out with these five verses, not reading or praying anything else. I would read it aloud as it was written, paraphrase it in prayer, and mediate on it as I awakened in the morning and when I went to sleep at night. These verses seemed to activate times of spiritual refreshment as I called on the Lord. Thus, we venture into these concepts presented in this scripture.

In this declaration of Christ, He presents many truths and insights into the will of the Father and into the desires of His heart. As in the previous chapters, we will dissect this scripture to comprehend it and receive as much as we can. With this, we are rooting ourselves deeper into the revelation of Christ, and as we meditate on these truths with the help of the Holy Spirit, I pray you come to know Christ more profoundly.

Verse 25-26: *At that time Jesus declared, "I thank you Father, Lord of heaven and earth, that you have hidden these things from the wise and understanding and revealed them to little children; yes, Father, for such was your gracious will.*

At the beginning of this declaration, Jesus thanks the Father for revealing the hidden things to "little children" according to His gracious will. What did Jesus mean by this? In Matthew 13:10-13, Scripture reveals to us just what He meant:

> *Then the disciples came and said to him, "Why do you speak to them in parables?" And he answered them, "To you it has been given to know the secrets of the kingdom of heaven, but to them it has not been given. For to the one who has, more will be given, and he will have an abundance, but from the one who has not, even what he has will be taken away. This is why I speak to them in parables, because seeing they do not see, and hearing they do not hear, nor do they understand.*

What Jesus is explaining here is the condition of the people amongst him. He explains to the disciples that it has been given to them to know the "hidden things" of the kingdom of heaven. The reason is because the people were only there "for the moment," but the disciples had drawn near to know Jesus, and because of this, they drew near the secrets of the kingdom. Now whether He was referring to their physical age or to their spiritual maturity, it can definitely be argued both ways, but as it shows in His declaration, the "little children" were separated from those He called "the wise and the understanding." A characteristic of the "little children" is that they are good at inquiring because their minds are open, and they have a faith that assures them that whatever the answer is must be the truth. In contrast, the "wise and prudent" will reason, question, and doubt, coming to some means of compromised knowledge to fit what they already know. Thus, we must apply ourselves to the heart of "little children" just as the disciples did, because there, God has ordered the secrets of the kingdom of heaven to be given.

Verse 27: *All things have been handed over to me by the Father, and no one knows the Son except the Father, and no one knows the Father except the Son and anyone whom the Son chooses to reveal him.*

Next, Jesus shifts His declaration and reveals the exclusiveness of His authority and intimacy with the Father. Basically, no one knows God like God. Jesus reveals that this simple fact has not changed after His incarnation. He is still God, and He has the authority to reveal Himself to whomever He desires. In the book of Hebrews, Scripture shares that the access to know God comes from Christ, as He gives us the power to when we draw near to God (Hebrews 7:25).

Christ will reveal the Father to anyone, sinner or saint, who desires to draw near to God through Him with a pure and sure heart! The Son reveals the Father to whom He has chosen, and He has chosen those who would dare to draw near to God through Him. As said in John 14:6-9:

> *Jesus said to him, "I am the way, and the truth, and the life. No one comes to the Father except through me. If you had known me, you would have known my Father also. From now on you do know him and have seen him. Philip said to him, "Lord, show us the Father, and it is enough for us." Jesus said to him, "Have I been with you so long, and you still do not know me, Philip? Whoever has seen me has seen the Father. How can you say, 'Show us the Father?' "*

Jesus is confronting the inquiry of His disciples and answer with a simple "if you know me, you know Him." To illustrate, if someone put my father and me next to each other and studied our characteristics and traits, they would probably say that I am just like my father. Scripture says that the fullness of God—His characteristic and traits—is pleased to dwell in Christ (Colossians 1:19).

God has put His splendor and majesty on display by Christ. He is one with the Son and the Spirit. This, we must understand by faith until we enter eternity. The Lord God, the God of Israel, is a triune Being: One, yet Three. When we see Jesus, we have seen the Father, and when we see and experience the Holy Spirit, He is the Father. Is that mystery not too deep for our hearts to fathom? To examine what Jesus was saying reiterates what we have already covered in previous chapters; we can only experience the heart of the Father through the Son giving us our papers of adoption, granting us the right to be children of God and know Him like He does!

Enter His Rest

Verse 28: Come to me, all who labor and are heavy laden, and I will give you rest.

Here, Jesus starts to call to the laborers and the heavy-laden. He invites them to Himself, that they may inherit rest as they increase their nearness to Him. He says, "Come to me." When we pray, we must remember this invitation. Hear the Lord calling out to you saying, "Come to me. You've worked and wandered all day with a lot on your shoulders. I will give you rest." The beauty in this verse is that the Greek term *anapauō* for "rest" means "to refresh," which means that being with Jesus is a total, undefiled, and unhindered rest (Strong's Greek Lexicon).

In Peter's message at the Temple, he states, "Repent therefore, and turn back, that your sins may be blotted out, that times of refreshing may come from the presence of the Lord" (Acts 3:19-20). This scripture tells us a great truth: that repentance means turning to the Lord and accepting the invitation of sanctification from Him. But what we forget many times is the second part of the process of repentance: refreshment. Indeed, God wants us to be upright, pure, and holy; He does not only want us to have a clear conscience because of our confession, but He also wants to refresh us in His presence, since being forgiven by God does not necessarily mean being refreshed by His presence. A holiness that is not sustained by the presence of God (or by the spiritual hunger for His presence) is not true holiness. Jesus is extending an invitation to us all. Let us hear Him before we pray; hear Him calling us to Himself, saying, "Come to me." And when we pray, let it be an acceptance of that invitation to enter into His rest.

When we pray, especially in our times of personal connection with the Lord, we should never need to have the mindset of struggle. Struggle or laborious prayer may be necessary in times of spiritual warfare but not in communion. But the struggle I am referring to is an internal struggle to connect. Many of us have a hard time getting into God's presence, and many of us strive to get a clear conscience by confessing our sins over and over. When I was younger, I struggled greatly with this mentality. I thought the more I prayed, the more I earned an audience with the Lord because I was proving myself to Him. But the Holy Spirit expressed to my heart that I am not earning His presence; I am simply receiving the invitation of Christ and drawing myself closer as I pray, as I worship, as I hear His voice in His word and as I live a holy life. When we pray, we are drawing near to the Lord to increase our relationship with Him. Jesus sets the tone of our meeting; when we come to the Lord, our goal should be the acceptance of His rest. As Hebrews 4:1-3 states,

> *Therefore, while the promise of entering his rest still stands, let us fear lest any of you should seem to have failed to reach it. For good news came to us just as to them, but the message they heard did not benefit them, because they were not united by faith with those who listened. For we who have believed enter that rest.*

We must never gain the mindset that the more we pray, the more we earn His presence, for it is something we can never *earn*. It is freely given, which makes our experience with the Lord even sweeter. To enter into the rest of His presence, we simply accept His invitation and draw near to the Lord in our hearts. With every move we make and every decision made to diligently seek Him, we are drawing closer to Him as we accept His beckoning. This restful dynamic of prayer expresses the power of believing, which God has simplified for us. It is complex to the flesh but simple in spirit; God wants us to believe and then come. If we do those two things, we will enter fully into His call of rest.

Put this book down again and say to Lord, "Here I am. I accept your invitation. Lord, You are my rest. I pray that I will enter into it right now." Wait on Him until you have received rest. If you feel any anxiety, ask the Holy Spirit to reveal any sin or worry that would hinder you from entering into it; then, confess and renounce them honestly and audibly. Finally, call upon the Lord again and enjoy being refreshed in His presence.

Rest Upon Me

Beloved, I hope you are enjoying the rest of His presence as we continue. I believe that many find only discontentment in their personal time with the Lord because they do not enter into His rest. Consequently, many of us struggle with various weights, worries, compromise, and sins because we do not receive the release of power to overcome them. Let us explore this concept by returning to His declaration in Matthew 11:

Verse 29: Take my yoke upon you and learn from me, for I am gentle and lowly in heart, and you will find rest for your souls.

The Lord broadens the terms of His invitation of rest, saying, "Take my yoke upon you and learn from me." When I first looked at this, I asked myself, what in the world is a yoke? A yoke is a harness, such as what horses pulling a carriage have upon their necks and backs. As I imagined the weight of a harness on my neck and back, I could not understand why Jesus would ever paint such a picture when desiring for us to rest. However, there are couple of insights to this verse that I believe will further our understanding of why Jesus uses this allegory.

Many of the people who were listening to Jesus' declaration of that time were farmers and people who were familiar with seeing oxen and a horse pulling carts or plows. They would be familiar with the process He was referencing, for what farmers would do was to fasten a young ox (for example) to a more experienced one so that the younger could learn from the older. When Jesus was giving this invitation, He might have been using this example to invite the people to come, yoke themselves to Him, and learn from His gentle and meek ways. If we do the same, as a result, we will find rest for our souls.

The word "yoke" also means "to bind or bond." When we come to the Lord daily and encounter His rest, we are bonding with a powerful person: meeting and receiving from the Almighty God. Jesus prayed in John 17:11 that we would become one with Him as He is one with the Father. Scripture shows us that Jesus many times went into desolate places to speak with the Father, and then He would enter a city, wielding the power to heal all diseases and cast out devils, displaying the power of God accompanied by the gospel of His kingdom. What we must be aware of at all times is that there is no power outside of fellowship with God; Jesus tells us continually that He did nothing from His own authority; He consulted and repeated everything he heard from His Father and did what He saw His Father do, finding His power through continually yoking Himself to the Father. How much more effective would we be as children of God if we yoked ourselves to Jesus daily, and by fellowship with Him received overcoming power to meet the standard of God?

I have heard countless times that "a man down before the Lord cannot fall." In those words, we will have the power to overcome the enticements of the world, of the flesh, and of the evil one if we busy ourselves in pleasing the Lord—and we please Him simply by following Him. Scripture records that Jesus called the disciples unto Himself (Matthew 10:1). There was no other reason for them to follow Him than to be close to Him, to learn from Him, and ultimately to represent Him in character and carry out His work on earth after His ascension. What Jesus wants us to do is not just follow, but to become His disciples: disciplined learners. We must make it a discipline in our lives to learn the ways of Jesus *from* Jesus.

Verse 30: For my yoke is easy and my burden is light.

Jesus explains to us that yoking ourselves with him is not burdensome. Christ lived in perpetual communion with the Father and it was from that place He was not defiled by the pleasures, pressures and burdens of this world. What if we had that same oneness with Christ? How wonderful would it to be enjoy living in the power like Him!

I have heard this deceptive concept of waiting until we are older to be with Christ, because many fear that His standard is too heavy according to the preference of our flesh. I have heard other young men say they will postpone the whole "Christianity deal" until they have fulfilled their carnal desires. I can tell you by deeply burning revelation that nothing will ever satisfy like God can. Jesus' yoke and His burden are far more enjoyable than the earthly passion we feel. In yoking ourselves to Jesus, we are being transformed to resemble Him on the earth, or as Paul states:

And we all, with unveiled face, beholding the glory of the Lord, are being transformed into the same image from one degree of glory to another. (2 Corinthians 3:18)

And through this companionship, we become eligible for an adventure full of glory.

Recap

Jesus has invited us to come to Him and find total rest, and when we seek a personal encounter with the Lord, we are accepting this invitation. Without it, we will continue to struggle with anxieties, sins, and compromise; only in enjoying His rest daily can we have the power to overcome every enticement of the world, of our flesh, and of the evil one. Lastly, know that only Christ can satisfy us. I encourage you to allow every aspect of your life to benefit from a heart fully satisfied by the Lord. As for me, I am giving everything to be like Him. Would you do the same?

I pray that your mind will be thrust into the mind sphere of faith, that you will enter into the rest of the Lord daily and bond with Him, inheriting the power to overcome the evil days ahead and to be like Him in the earth. I pray that your heart will ever hunger for an audience with Him and will remain in hot pursuit of His ways. I bless you to go and pursue the Lord: in Jesus' Name.

CHAPTER 5

Intimacy With The Holy Spirit

Our Greatest Friend

I hope that as you read this book, the Lord is encountering you on a daily basis. I pray that your faith and hope is revitalized and your heart is filled with a deeper hunger for the splendor of God. Ask continually for the Lord to open your mind and enlighten your heart to receive insight.

Within this chapter, we will explore why it is important to know the Holy Spirit intimately. I will not be arguing pneumatology, for Scripture is clear. I have experienced that the Holy Spirit is who Scripture teaches us He is. He is a person, not an animated force or wind. He speaks and has a mind, feelings, and will (Hebrews 3:7; 1 Timothy 4:1; Romans 8:27, 15:30; 1 Corinthians 12:11). He is fully God; He is the Spirit of God; He is the first person of the Godhead who was revealed in Scripture (Genesis 1:2). He is of equal importance with the Son and the Father. As a matter of fact, Scripture tells us He is the Spirit of the Father (Matthew 10:20), and He is the Spirit of Jesus, the Son (Philippians 1:19). He has been my friend since I was twelve years of age, and I have experienced that He is tender, meek, yet to be revered and honored. His purpose is to teach us about Jesus and to lead us into the truth of His Word; He is the One who wrote the Bible through the inspired words He gave to His chosen scribes.

Without the Holy Spirit, there is no Scripture, no Church, and no power. He is the Spirit of Christ who leads the Church (Acts 1:8), the dispenser of all the spiritual gifts listed in Scripture (Romans 12:3-8, 1 Corinthians 12:1-13), and the Helper of the saints (John 14:15-17, 16:7). He inspires conviction and is the power of God in the earth (John 16:8-11, Matthew 12:28). He is holy and altogether beautiful. Without Him there is no salvation, because without Him there is no power to the Gospel (1 Corinthians 12:3).

The Holy Spirit is a gift (Acts 2:38-39). Without Him, there is no experiencing God through Christ (John 16:7-8, 13-15). Without Him, this book would have never been in your hands. For a more in-depth manuscript focusing solely on the Holy Spirit, John Bevere's recent book, *The Holy Spirit: An Introduction*, is worth reading. Now, let us refresh our hearts on how important it is to know the Holy Spirit.

Jesus blessed His disciples with fundamental understandings of the Holy Spirit's ministry in the New Testament. Scripture records these descriptions:

> *If you love me, you will obey my commandments. And I will ask the Father, and he will give you another Helper, to be with you forever, even the Spirit of truth, whom the world cannot receive, because it neither sees him nor knows him. You know him, for he dwells with you and will be in you.* (John 14:15-17)

Later in the same chapter, it continues:

> *But the Helper the Holy Spirit, whom the Father will send in my name, he will teach you all things and bring to your remembrance all that I have said to you.* (John 14:26)

Finally, Jesus speaks on His departure, saying that a Helper would come in His place:

> *Nevertheless, I tell you the truth: it is to your advantage that I go away, for if I do not go away, the Helper will not come to you. But if I go, I will send him to you. And when he comes, he will convict the world concerning sin and righteousness and judgment. When the Spirit of truth comes, he will guide you into all the truth, for he will not speak on His own authority, but whatever he hears he will speak, and he will declare to you the things that are to come. He will glorify, for he will take what is mine and declare it to you. All that the Father has is mine, therefore I said that he will take what is mine and declare it to you.* (John 16:7-8, 13-15)

We will unpack these scriptures to better magnify the importance of the Holy Spirit:

1. *If you love me, you will obey my commandments.*

Jesus begins His introduction to personal intimacy with the Holy Spirit by encourage the disciples obedience to flow from love for Him. He then reveals to them the reward of this love.

2. *And I will ask the Father, and He will give you another Helper, to be with you forever, even the Spirit of Truth.*

After Jesus admonishes His disciples in love, the source of obedience, He then promises them an amazing relationship with His guide and friend. I have heard many teachings regarding the translation of the word "Helper"; the Greek term "*paraklētos*" means "counselor, intercessor, comforter, helper, encourager, and advocate" (Strong's Greek Lexicon). If that description is applied, the Holy Spirit is the greatest friend in the world!

To clarify, we are not His friends just for the duration of our earthly experience, and then when we get to eternity, our entire relational equity is reserved for Jesus. Truly, life in eternity will be about the Glory of God shown by His Son, but only through knowing the Holy Spirit can we capture such glory, and it is through the Holy Spirit that Christ is revealed. We must know what the Holy Spirit is in relationship with Him. The Spirit gives us direction and counsel, intercedes with Christ for us and with, even through us. He is our comfort in good times and bad, and our helper in weakness and strength. He will always encourage us when we are discouraged, and He will fight as an advocate for us at any moment!

What a glorious reality! Jesus is at the right hand of the Father, interceding and fighting for us, and the Holy Spirit is our friend, doing the same work and more. So much of our relationship with the Holy Spirit is found in this one word, "helper." It sounds very simple, but this life in Christ will only go as far as our relationship with the Holy Spirit.

3. *Who the world cannot receive, because it neither knows Him.*

Jesus then reveals to us that this relationship is not for the world—that is, those who have not drawn near to Him. There is nothing like enjoying an exclusive relationship with the Holy Spirit. There are many even in the Church who are in category of the world, because they do not know Him. Those of the world cannot receive the Holy Spirit, this great friendship, because they do not know how amazing He is. If all of us in the Church knew the Holy Spirit, this contentment with Sunday-morning Christianity and lukewarm prayer lives would never even be a reality!

4. *You know him, for he dwells with you and will be in you.*

"But you know him," Jesus says with a tone of assurance. Not you *will* know Him, or you will *come* to know Him. Could this be the introduction of a wonderful hope and promised friendship with the Holy Spirit? Jesus answers it by saying, "For He dwells with you and will be in you." The disciples were very familiar with Jesus' actions, and Scripture credits the Holy Spirit for helping Him release the kingdom of heaven into the earth. Jesus, in the gospel of Matthew, states, "But if it is by the Spirit of God that I cast out demons, then the kingdom of God has come upon you" (Matthew 12:28). What a revelation! Jesus, through the ministry of the Holy Spirit, could operate and release the power, order, and authority of the kingdom of heaven, so the disciples were well acquainted with the works of the Spirit through Christ. Now, He was promising them a relationship with His Helper, the one who led Him, spoke to Him the words of the Father, and enlightened His human heart to understand His will. They even experienced the Holy Spirit for themselves and received and spoke revelation from the Holy Spirit.

Jesus also said that He will be in us. When you have a best friend, you know that person so well, it is almost as if you can operate as them at any given time. When you are with a friend, you consistently pour into each other—your life, your character, your likes and dislikes, etc. This is our relationship with the Holy Spirit. We are invited to know Him as a friend; then, we will cease seeing Him as just the power to barely live this Christ-won life and expect to get into heaven. Heaven is here and now; open your eyes! We experience the love of the Father and the grace of Jesus by the Holy Spirit; there is no one in the world that can love and be a friend to us like Him! Let it be said of us in eternity that we intimately know the Holy Spirit.

Jesus said that the Spirit would lead and guide us into all truth; if we want to know about anything, He will bring us into the truth. We literally have access to a person who made everything and knows everything! We would be the best entrepreneurs if we truly were in a relationship with the only person who knows everything! Talk about wealth and world reformation coming through the Church! The Church would help nations get out of debt if we simply knew the Holy Spirit! We can walk in a continual state of knowing exactly what to do, because our great friend knows everything and we inquire of Him.

Jesus went as far as to say that "it is to your advantage that I go, so that the Holy Spirit can come." If the resurrected Jesus was still here, we probably would not have an intimate relationship with Him. We would probably keep up with Him with His miracles and such on television, but it would be impossible to truly have a relationship. Jesus left so that what He was limited to do in flesh, the Eternal Spirit not bound by time, space, or quantity could do as He is doing in the earth today.

The finished work of the cross is important, and its message is the cause of the Kingdom, but there is no message powerful enough to change the heart of men without the powerful aid of the Holy Spirit. And Jesus did say we will have not only a mentor and a guide, but also a glorious friend to know intimately. So when we pray, we should always be aware of the Helper's presence, direction, and heart as a friend.

The Power of Fellowship

Paul the apostle, finishing His second letter to the Corinthians, states, "The grace of the Lord Jesus Christ and the love of God and the fellowship of the Holy Spirit be with you all." (2 Corinthians 13:14 ESV). What caught my eyes is what it says at the end: "the fellowship of the Holy Spirit be with you all." For some reason my heart leapt as I read those words, because the word "fellowship" means, "to have a friendly association with someone." What would fellowship with the Holy Spirit look like? What would it be like to walk in consistent fellowship with the one dwelling on the inside of you? This can be described in one word: power. Jesus said in Acts 1:8, "But you will receive power when the Holy Spirit has come upon you." When we fellowship with the Holy Spirit, what we experience in our day to day experience will almost seem like power flowing through our veins. There are many powerless Christians who enjoy Sunday mornings and playing patty-cake with God once in a while, but then there are those who seem to walk with a confidence yet meekness, and there is something unique about them; it even seems like they know something that everyone else does not. Power.

It is very evident that fellowship with the Holy Spirit was a profound staple in the early Church. As we read the book of Acts, the Godhead who showed up the most, actively leading the apostles and early churches, was the Holy Spirit. In verses like Acts 4:31, His activity is shown: "And when they had prayed, the place in which they were gathered together was shaken, and they were all filled with the Holy Spirit and continued to speak the word of God with boldness." When Stephen stood in the synagogue, those who disputed with him "could not withstand the wisdom and the Spirit with which he was speaking" (Acts 6:10). Acts 10:44 has another potent example: "While Peter was still saying these things, the Holy Spirit fell on all who heard the word." And because the apostles worked so many signs, wonders, and miracles, the people would even lay the sick in the streets to be healed as the shadow of Peter passed over them (Acts 5:12-16). The teachers of the Antioch Church, seeking direction of what to do with Saul and Barnabas, state, "While they were worshipping the Lord and fasting, the Holy Spirit said, 'Set apart for me Barnabas and Saul for the work to which I have called them' " (Acts 13:2).

Now Paul, a Church persecutor turned apostle, did not personally walk with Jesus on the earth. Perhaps we could say that while the 11 who started it all were apostles of the Lamb, Paul was an apostle of the Holy Spirit, for it was through the Holy Spirit that he knew Jesus. Peter praises Paul for revealing so many mysteries and bringing forth order in many churches, because Paul had been given great revelatory power through his consistent fellowship with the Holy Spirit. When we read the book of Acts, we see that "God was doing extraordinary miracles by the hands of Paul, so that even handkerchiefs or aprons that had touched his skin were carried to the sick, and their diseases left them and the evil spirits came out of them" (Acts 19:11-12). And through Paul, the Holy Spirit spread His revelation even further.

What an amazing result of fellowship with the Holy Spirit. The apostles and early church had the power to preach the good news of the kingdom of Heaven with boldness and immovable faith, and they took to heart what Jesus had said of the Holy Spirit, our Helper, and taught others about Him. The Holy Spirit has not changed; the same power that came through the disciples due to their fellowship with Him is the same power that can flow through us today if we pursue what the Lord has revealed to us about the Holy Spirit.

If you have been struggling with prayer, sin, moral compromise, or even depression, or pain in your body, invite the Holy Spirit in and fellowship with Him. Many times, the disciples experienced the Holy Spirit in Acts when they prayed. In order for the Holy Spirit to show up, they must have been praying for Him or even praying Him in. Ask the Father to fill you and your life with the Holy Spirit. Invite Him continually and ask for His help. The Holy Spirit loves you; as a matter of fact, the Father has sent Him to shed His love into your heart, and He is the grace and power of Jesus in the earth today. Paul stated, "The grace of the Lord Jesus Christ and the love of God and the fellowship of the Holy Spirit be with you all" (2 Corinthians 13:14), and we have solidified the grace of Jesus and of the Father by the Spirit's ministry. May you accept His gift.

The Freedom of Knowing

Lastly, there are three segments of Romans 8 that I would like to use as foundational scriptures to explain to you what I mean by "the freedom of knowing." I encourage you to read the entire chapter, for I refer to it several times. Let us discuss these scriptures to enlighten our hearts to see the freedom of knowing:

For those who live according to the flesh set their minds on things of the flesh, but those who live according to the Spirit set their minds on the things of the Spirit. For to set the mind on the flesh is death, but to set the mind on the Spirit is life and peace. (Romans 8:5-6)

In these two verses, Paul describes the state of mind of those who live according to the Spirit, and those who live according to the flesh. I believe these are the days when the Lord is correcting this sense of entitlement in the Church and reforming our carnal "Christianity" and reestablishing Spirit-led Christianity. As believers in Christ, we are encouraged by the Scripture, living under the law of the Spirit of life, to set our minds on the "things of the Spirit" to reap the life and peace we are to inherit. Jesus, in the book of John, promises that He has come to give us abundant life and leave with us His peace (John 10:10). Thus, we find out that the life and peace that is promised to be our inheritance comes solely from the Spirit. My next question would be, "What are the things of the Spirit?" In 1 Corinthians 2:9-11, this question is answered:

But, as it is written, "What no eye has seen, nor ear heard, nor the heart of man imagined, what God has prepared for those who love Him"—these things God has revealed to us through the Spirit. For the Spirit searches everything, even the depths of God. For who knows a person's thoughts except the spirit of that person, which is in him? So also no one comprehends the thoughts of God except the Spirit of God."

The things of the Spirit are the thoughts of God, which are the secrets, wisdom, insights, counsels, and revelations of His heart and kingdom. This passage tells us that the Spirit is here to reveal the very thoughts of the Holy One. We do not have to guess what the Lord is thinking, feeling or doing; we simply set our minds on Him and live in the life and peace provided through that continual exchange. What a glorious actuality, that we can know the thoughts of God! Have you ever wondered what God is thinking in heaven right now about you, your life, the nations, and the Church? You no longer have to imagine it for yourself—the Spirit of God is here to free us from wandering aimlessly, guessing and grappling with our thoughts of God's will. We can know His mind *now*, by the Holy Spirit.

Furthermore, Romans 8 adds on another fold to the Holy Spirit's intimate indwelling. Verses 14-17 encourages us that we know we have truly stepped into our divine sonship, when our lives and hearts are led by the Spirit of God:

For all who are led by the Spirit are sons of God. For you did not receive the spirit of slavery to fall back into fear, but you have received the Spirit of adoption as sons, by whom we cry, "Abba, Father!" The Spirit himself bears witness with our spirit that we are children of God, and if children, then heirs—heirs of God and fellow heirs with Christ.

Can you believe there are those that call themselves "Christians," yet because they reject the holistic leadership and presence of the Holy Spirit, are hindered from entering into the fullness of their God-given sonship? Scripture further states that it is by the Spirit of God that we can cry out to God as our Father. When Christians are not living in our sonship identity, we are rejecting the entire reason for the cross. God does not desire that we experience Him as Father only when we get to heaven; He has sent His Spirit to live within us—if we will receive Him—and now, erupting from our spirits is a longing that breaks out into a cry to our Father. When we experientially know the holistic leadership of the Holy Spirit, we are freed from all that has hindered us from knowing our Creator as our Father. We are freed in knowing that we are sons and daughters of life and peace, not slaves of fear and condemnation. For when the Spirit leads us, a deep conviction lies within that knows: the Holy God of Eternity is my Father.

Lastly, let us return to Romans 8:26-27. We have studied it before, but let us review it briefly to refresh our memories:

> *Likewise the Spirit helps us in our weakness. For we do not know what to pray for as we ought, but the Spirit himself intercedes for us with groanings too deep for words. And he who searches hearts knows what is the mind of the Spirit, because the Spirit intercedes for the saints according to the will of God.*

As the passage shows, without the Holy Spirit, our Helper, we do not know how or even what we ought to pray. However, we can fully trust that the Holy Spirit will enlighten our eyes, and there will come from our bellies a groan filled with petition that words are not able to communicate. We are freed in knowing that the Holy Spirit will teach us and help us to pray. He will open up our spirits to His thoughts, and from that place, Scripture says that He will intercede on our behalf according to the will of God. Rest assured that God understands sighs, groans, and tears. Because of the Holy Spirit's dwelling inside of us, we know that we will walk in complete fulfillment of God's will for our lives.

Recap

The Holy Spirit is the greatest friend we could ever ask for. He gives us direction and counsel and intercedes with Christ for us and with us; He is our comfort whether in good times or trouble, and He is our helper in our weaknesses and strength. He will always be here to encourage us and fight for us at any moment! Fellowshipping with Him provides the power to know Christ and to live this life in God-purposed fullness. We receive direction, counsel, wisdom, insight, and the boldness we need to be witnesses of His loving message to the world. We are free in knowing that when we do not know how or even what to pray, the Spirit of God is our help in our times of weakness, even making our silent sighs, groans, and tears more expressive than words. Finally, because of the Spirit of God infiltrating every aspect of our life, we possess the freedom of knowing the thoughts and emotions of God and the revelation of Christ. We are free as He enlightens us to our identity as sons and daughters of God and brothers and sisters of Jesus to walk in the security and power of our divine adoption.

I pray that you will get addicted to intimately knowing and fellowshipping with the Holy Spirit. Ask Him to come and partner with you, to be your friend and guide, and ask Him to make you sensitive to His promptings, whispers, and small inward impressions. I pray He answers with the weight and power of His presence. I pray that His presence will begin to wash over the atmosphere of your heart like a tsunami overtaking the seashore.

CHAPTER 6

Partnership with the Holy Spirit

The Ministry of the Holy Spirit

The Holy Spirit's work in the earth is to lead the embassy of the kingdom (The Church) and usher us into eternity with God. What we see many times is the lack of understanding that this ministry that we are a part of is not our ministry to lead. It is the ministry of the Holy Spirit. The preaching of the Gospel without the Holy Spirit is powerless and does not cause eternal change in anyone's lives—not the world's, and not ours. We are partakers of the ministry of the Lord Jesus through the leadership, power and lordship of the Holy Spirit in the world. Paul, comparing the OT with the NT, states in 2 Corinthians 3:7-8:

> *Now the ministry of death, carved in letters on stone, came with such glory that the Israelites could not gaze at Moses' face because of its glory, which was being brought to an end, will not the ministry of the Spirit have even more glory?*

Scripture acknowledges that the New Covenant of Christ is under the ministry of the Holy Spirit. Paul before this letter writes, "Therefore I want you to understand that no one speaking in the Spirit of God ever says 'Jesus is accursed!' and no one can say "Jesus is Lord" except in the Holy Spirit" (1 Corinthians 12:3). Thus, we also know that the salvation the New Covenant was set in place to provide comes only through the ministry of the Holy Spirit. The Lord Jesus founded the New Covenant by the help and power of the Holy Spirit, and it is by that same Spirit that we come to know, believe, and partake of this New Covenant with God. Scripture also says it like this:

> *But when the goodness and loving kindness of God our Savior appeared, he saved us, not because of works done by us in righteousness, but according to his own mercy, by the washing of regeneration and renewal of the Holy Spirit, whom he poured out on us richly through Jesus Christ our Savior, so that being justified by his grace we might become heirs according to the hope of eternal life.* (Titus 3:4-7)

Our sanctification was made available by the cross, but it is provided by and through the ministry of the Holy Spirit. As is written in 2 Corinthians 5:17-21:

> *Therefore, if anyone is in Christ, he is a new creation. The old has passed away; behold, the new has come. All this is from God, who through Christ reconciled us to himself and gave us the ministry of reconciliation; that is, in Christ God was reconciling the world to himself, not counting their trespasses against them, and entrusting to us the message of reconciliation. Therefore, we are ambassadors for Christ, God making his appeal through us. We implore you on behalf of Christ, be reconciled to God. For our sake he made him to be sin who knew no sin, so that in him we might become the righteousness of God.*

This scripture, which is a part of the foundation of our ministry and confession of sanctification, never once mentioned the name "Jesus," but consistently referred to Him as Christ, meaning Anointed One; thus, Jesus without the anointing, which we know to be the Holy Spirit, could have never been the "Christ" who provided salvation, sanctification, righteousness, and power for us! Without the Holy Spirit, the assignment of Jesus to the cross could have never been done. It was the Holy Spirit who placed Jesus in Mary's womb, and it was the Holy Spirit who came upon Him at His baptism; by the Holy Spirit, He was led by the Father; and by the Holy Spirit, He had the power to perform miracles and cast out evil spirits. It was only by the Holy Spirit that He was able to endure even to the cross, and it was by the Holy Spirit He was resurrected! Hence, I do not understand why we in the 21st century Church displace the Holy Spirit's importance and lordship in our lives, for as is written in 2 Corinthians 3:16-18:

> *But when one turns to the Lord, the veil is removed. Now the Lord is the Spirit, and where the Spirit of the Lord is, there is freedom. And we all, with unveiled face, beholding the glory of the Lord, are being transformed into the same image from one degree of glory to another. For this comes from the Lord who is the Spirit.*

John Bevere provides a rephrase that may enlighten us: "Wherever the Spirit is Lord; that's where there is freedom" (Bevere 5).

We see many churches that have great doctrinal presentations, soul-satisfying worship sets, decent hand-raisers, and programs that reach out to the homeless and the destitute, but without our ministries being partakers of the ministry of the Spirit, we are committing spiritual self-satisfaction and are cheating ourselves out of the powerful impact we are meant to have as ambassadors of Christ on the earth.

I have belabored this topic so that we can understand that if we are not submitted and yielded to the Holy Spirit and His leadership and lordship over the Church, we will cheapen our salvation as a Sunday-morning fling and leave our grace to be witnesses to bumper stickers. We will deceive ourselves into thinking our theological prayers are effective in our lives without the Holy Spirit inspiring and empowering them according to the will of God. We will make lukewarm our walk with Christ because we, like the world, refuse and reject the governance and power of the Holy Spirit. Beloved, if we try to reach to the uttermost world with the Gospel without first waiting on and praying for the Holy Spirit to take lordship over our ministries, we are only fooling ourselves if we think our human efforts can infiltrate nations when we do not have the true power to show them the reality of Christ. We will continue to see gimmicks, campaigns, and carnal ideas being employed in an effort to add numbers to the Church.

The difference between us and the early Church, which was under the leadership and lordship of the Holy Spirit, is that they performed miracles, signs, and wonders, and because of His favor, people were added to the Church daily. What would it look like if the Church in all the nations submitted to the lordship of the Holy Spirit? Furthermore, what would we look like in our prayer experience if we, *individually*, did the same?

The Struggle and Miracle of Prayer

Beloved, do you know that to pray in our days is a struggle? The Lord directs us in this matter, saying:

> *But when you pray, go into your room and shut the door and pray to your Father who is in secret. And your Father who sees in secret will reward you.* (Matthew 6:6)

Here, the Lord says, "WHEN we pray," not "*if* we pray." He entreats us to go before Him in secret. We know it is for the purpose that we may lay bare before the Lord with meek and lowly hearts, not trying to impress others like hypocrites. But if we take this scripture and apply it to the 21st century culture with all its technology and advances, we are filled with persistent distractions. If we go into our rooms, we are facing the distractions of our phones receiving texts and calls or our minds going off to wander about dinner. Our Facebook, Twitter, Instagram, and Pinterest are all calling our names. We have school and work to worry about, or we have families that keep interrupting. Our attention spans are like bees in the middle of a field of flowers, our minds buzzing from one thing to the next.

At that point we think, "Oh, maybe some worship music will help"; then we struggle to figure out whether to put on Bethel Music or Jesus Culture. We finally pick an instrumental and try to quiet ourselves, but everything that has entertained our hearts since last week keeps bothering us, and we walk away unsatisfied with our prayer life, many times giving up. In moments like this, "WHEN you pray" becomes more like an "*if* you pray." Next, we slip in and out of compromise and in and out of shame; it is almost like we are creating sin! Soon, we are in and out of condemnation and in and out of depression. Finally, we just give up on the whole thing and wonder if this Christianity deal is even worth our exasperation. Many begin to seek something other than God because they could not overcome the struggle of prayer—the inward battle of distraction, aimlessness and frustration. This is a vivid example, because I have lived it! Like many others, I could have avoided this situation if I had yielded myself totally to the leadership and lordship of the Holy Spirit.

Beloved, I will say this again; without the Holy Spirit, our prayer attempts are in vain. Without His guidance, help, and power, our prayers are lukewarm in heart, dry, and ineffective, because genuine prayer is found as we yield ourselves to Him. I assure you that you can overcome this struggle by three seemingly simple practices: start with the Spirit, walk by the Spirit, and proceed in the Spirit:

1. Start with the Spirit

As I have said before, we all share a weakness, and that is in the area of prayer, for as Romans 8:26 states, "We do not know what to pray for as we ought." Or, when it seems like we *should* know what to pray, we do not. However, before Scripture addresses our weaknesses, it encourages us by saying that the Holy Spirit is here to help.

The Spirit functions in many ways, some of which are provided in Isaiah 11:2:

> *And the Spirit of the Lord shall rest upon him, the Spirit of wisdom and understanding, the Spirit of counsel and might, the Spirit of knowledge and the fear of the Lord.*

When we start by calling for and waiting on the Holy Spirit to aid us, we gain all these benefits. We step into wisdom and understanding, counsel and power, the knowledge of the Holy One, and the fear of the Lord. When I started dedicating myself to prayer, I would burst out, calling for the Holy Spirit, beckoning Him to come and help me. This "come," I later understood, was not a "come because You are not here" type of invitation, but a "come increase Your manifested nearness so that You can help start this wheel turning." Now, many times I would do this, and distractions would still come up. I would begin to shut them out by again and again, calling for the Holy Spirit's help to be totally concentrated on the Father. Whispered phrases like "Help me Holy Spirit" would be released as I sought to truly be focused on the Lord as I prayed.

Even the needs of our flesh can distract from getting deeper into prayer; as Jesus says to His sleepy disciples at the time of prayer in the garden before His betrayal:

> *Watch and pray that you may not enter into temptation. The spirit indeed is willing, but the flesh is weak.* (Matthew 26:41)

With this verse, Jesus shows us how to overcome and not enter into the enticement of our flesh. Many times we feel an urgency and willingness to pray, but because of the weakness of the flesh, we fall into its enticement. When starting to pray, avoid jumping directly to your needs, wants, or notions of what you think are "deep enough" to be uttered. Wait until you know the anointing of the Holy Spirit is upon you, or it seems like words or melodies are bubbling up inside of you. Many times, I would pray, "Open my heart to sense your leading, Holy Spirit." Prayer may start in worship and in singing praises to God from our hearts, whether in words we understand, or a song from our spirits. As Scripture teaches us,

> *Enter his gates with thanksgiving, and his courts with praise! Give thanks to him; bless his name!* (Psalm 100:4)

When we come before a king, we do not unload our problems immediately, but we first pay sincere homage. We have to remember that Scripture tells us that we are going before the Lord in the throne of grace (Hebrews 4:16). We are meeting with the King, and the only way to enter with grace is when we are led by the Holy Spirit, who may at times lead us into a chorus of spiritual songs from our hearts. As stated in Jeremiah 33:3:

> *Call to me and I will answer you, and will tell you great and hidden things that you have not known.*

If we simply call and wait on the Holy Spirit, we will start in prayer the right way and enter the presence and rest of God.

2. Walk by the Spirit

After perceiving the Holy Spirit's help and feeling His presence in our space, this helps the eyes of our hearts to be enlightened and our gazes to be fixed on the Father. Scripture tells us in Galatians 5:16, "But I say, walk by the Spirit, and you will not gratify the desires of the flesh." It continues in verse 25, "If we live by the Spirit, let us also keep in step with the Spirit." Now, since His presence has filled our space and we feel His power to pray, we must not wander off praying in the flesh—the un-renewed weakness of our minds. If we begin to pray in the flesh, we begin to return back to the place of weakness that the Holy Spirit has come to help us out of. Therefore, the only way to avoid this situation is to keep in step with the Spirit.

I liken prayer to walking in the night. When we are walking alone, insecurities, fears and panic can overcome us quickly; but when we are walking with a strong friend, we feel more at rest, and it is a joyous occasion as we keep in step with the strength of our friend. The Holy Spirit is our strong friend in the walk of prayer; without Him, we are like people walking blindly in the dark; we keep fumbling and bumbling around hopelessly. So when the Holy Spirit enters into your space, take Him by the hand and walk with Him step by step as He leads you. Do not feel the need to always say something in prayer; allow Him to quiet you so you can bask in His presence.

In Western culture, we live in a mindset that if we are not busy, we are not progressing. But Scripture teaches us, "In returning and rest you shall be saved; in quietness and in trust shall be your strength" (Isaiah 30:15). The beauty of the leading of the Holy Spirit is that He is like a shepherd, leading you only where you need to be. This is well-illustrated in Psalm 23:2-3, which says, "He leads me beside still waters. He restores my soul." At other times, He wants you to bombard the throne room with praise and loud proclamations. Do not be afraid to do that either. The Bible says that in prison, Paul and Silas lifted up their voices and began to pray and sing hymns so that the whole prison heard them! Then the ground began to shake and their bonds were loosed (Acts 16:25-26). Many times, you may not know why the Holy Spirit is leading you to do certain things, but if you obey His leading, you will witness the heavens open over your life, and you will be more than satisfied. He may lead you to sit, walk or kneel—whichever it is, remain in step with Him.

How do you know the Holy Spirit is leading you? When one's heart is enlightened, you will just know. It is like a knowing beyond your intelligence. Many times, you will just know what to pray, and a sense of affirmation and fulfillment will arise in your heart. When this becomes less frequent, yield more of yourself until you get back into the freedom of knowing. Beloved, rest assured that you will simply just know.

3. Proceed in the Spirit

When the rhythm is going, move with it. Allow the Holy Spirit to sweep you up and experience what He will have for you. Being careful to proceed and making sure your flesh is not getting in the way is probably the most important thing to do in private prayer. Move by faith, trusting that what your spirit is receiving is coming from the leading witness of the Holy Spirit. Just proceed.

An amazing test is when you pray, write it down and see if what you prayed is in Scripture, a truth of your life, or something that will come to pass in the future. When I started to do this, I did not know that most of what I was praying applied to parts of Scripture I was not even aware of. It amazed and encouraged me in my prayer walk. This is the miracle of prayer: that by the Holy Spirit, we overcome the distractions, aimlessness, and frustration that can distract us from His fellowship.

The Acceleration of Time

You may think this process takes forever. To be honest, at first, it seems to. When I started these interlaced practices, I would spend three to four hours in prayer to make sure that I was being patient with it. I would not proceed to say or do anything unless I knew in my gut the Holy Spirit was manifested. And as time went by, I could almost instantly pray out the will of God in confidence without the hours and hours of pressing into a weighty audience with the Holy Spirit. As I matured, I had the confidence in the ever-present help of the Holy Spirit, and He seemed as a consistent stream flowing in me. I could accomplish in less than 30 minutes what once took me 4 hours; in an hour, it seemed like I produced the same fruit of what then seemed to take me a day before the Lord. Now do not get me wrong—I loved every minute of those four hours. At times, I would spend days in prayer in the presence of the Holy Spirit. I would be spending time with my family watching television, and I would feel the Holy Spirit calling me to pray. I would run to my room because there was nothing to me like praying with the Holy Spirit, and the glory of God would fill my room for days. I would fall to my knees or my face because of the weight of His nearness. But as I grew in the knowledge of the Lord and increased in stature, wisdom, and responsibility, the Lord graced my 30-second prayer with the potency of 30 minutes. I call it the acceleration of time.

To express this idea of acceleration, I found in the gospel of John a declaration of Jesus. To the woman at the well, Scripture records:

> *Jesus said to her, "Everyone who drinks of this water will be thirsty again, but whoever drinks of the water that I will give him will never be thirsty again. The water that I will give him will become in him a spring of water welling up to eternal life." (John 4:13-14)*

Jesus states that we will first drink of His given water, but then that same water will become—like in the process of maturity—a spring welling up within. When I was younger in prayer, I ran to my room to drink from the well of the Spirit, but as I became more and more acquainted with Him, it became like a spring inside of me that could well up almost instantly. Jesus even furthers this same revelation later on in the gospel of John, stating:

> *"If anyone thirsts, let him come to me and drink. Whoever believes in me, as the Scripture has said, 'Out of his heart will flow rivers of living water.' " Now this he said about the Spirit, whom those who believed in him were to receive, for as yet the Spirit had not been given, because Jesus was not yet glorified.* (John 7:37-39)

The "water" that Jesus spoke of is the Holy Spirit. Once we begin to drink from the Spirit consistently, He will increasingly begin to flow through us like rivers of living water from our hearts. In my prayer, I once had to repeat many times, "Holy Spirit, help me to pray," but as I continue to grow and increase in the Lord, that prayer lessens into an unspoken confidence and assurance of faith in the Holy Spirit's empowerment. Supernatural advancement in the experiential knowledge of God is the key to acceleration of time in prayer.

Wisdom means, "The quality of having experience, knowledge, and good judgement; the quality of being wise " ("Wisdom" def. 7). When the Spirit of wisdom comes upon you, He increases in you the knowledge of the Lord, and you will become skillful in prayer. You can utter one word, and the heavens will move on your behalf.

This must be our aspiration: to become so close to the Lord that it takes the snap of a finger to connect and keep in step with the Holy Spirit, and by that consistent flow with Him, we will be able to accomplish in days what once took generations to accomplish. The nearness of the coming of Christ requires this. Gone are the days of fiddling our thumbs in the place of prayer; we must yield and yield and yield some more until we are totally in sync with the Holy Spirit.

Recap

We are not the lords of the Church; we are partakers and partners in the ministry of the Holy Spirit. We must return to the power released by us submitting ourselves to His leadership and lordship. The struggle of prayer is the inward battle of weakness, distraction, aimlessness, and ultimately frustration and discontentment; how we overcome it is by starting with the Holy Spirit, keeping in step with Him, and being careful to proceed in Him above all things, and as we mature and increase in the experiential knowledge of the Lord by the Spirit, we will accomplish in moments what once took us hours. If we will simply be patient in the process, we can reap the benefit of doing in days what once took generations.

I pray that the Lord uniquely shapes the application of this knowledge in your life and that these things will increasingly show themselves faithful and sure. Pray this with me: Father, forgive me if I neglected Your Spirit in my heart, for it has caused my works to be dead and my labor to be in vain. I repent of and turn from those ways, and I yield my heart to Your Spirit. I submit to you. I thank You for Him and receive Him as my most precious gift. Holy Spirit, I invite You to come even closer. Help me to pray and increase Your presence and activity in my life. Help me to keep in step with You. Dwell in me, and may my heart be sensitive to Your leading and aware at all times of Your lordship. Awaken me to Your promptings and help me to obey at all times. In Jesus' name, amen.

With All Prayer

In Ephesians 6, Paul opens our minds to the arsenal of weapons we can wield against the evil of this world, and he charges us to continue to "[pray] at all times in the Spirit, with all prayer and supplication. To that end keep alert with all perseverance, making supplication for all the saints" (Ephesians 6:18 ESV). Many have interpreted "praying at all times in the Spirit" to mean "pray all the time," but I propose this paradigm: that Paul is telling us that every time we pray, we must be in the control of the Spirit. In the previous chapters, we have already covered what it means to pray by the leading of the Holy Spirit, so we do not need to belabor those insights. I would like to focus on the phrase in this scripture that we will examine, which states, "with all prayer and supplication." This indicates to us that there must be different types of prayer. Without this understanding, we as the Church have become familiar with only one type of prayer. For example, one church may only be comfortable singing out their prayers in a hymnal or spiritual style, while another may only feel comfortable with silent prayers. What we lack with such a mindset is the effectiveness we would have if we engaged in all prayer. We have already solidified what prayer is, and to refresh your memory, these are our five statements of prayer:

- Prayer shown in Scripture boils down to a simple definition: to ask or call to someone with a need or desire.
- Prayer is generally a vocal practice.
- Prayer is a dialogue, a call and response, a beckoning of one another (generally man to God).
- Prayer is an inward interaction of soul (mind, will and emotions) and spirit, laying hold of the willing human finitude as a sacrifice to the eternal God, to reach an intended state of being.
- Prayer is, at its core, the satisfying of the true internal burning of a flawed humanity to commune with the One and Only Perfect God.

With this defined platform, we lay a foundation for prayer in many ways. Each concept involves mostly individual prayer, but it is also a sound foundation for all prayer Therefore, the question is, what is "all prayer?" I believe Paul was referring to various things in this scripture. He first says that every time we pray, we must make sure it is in the Spirit—and we know that the Holy Spirit's leading in prayer will lead us in what we must pray. Next, we see in the study of Scripture different streams of prayer such as personal prayer, corporate prayer, intercession, prayers of spiritual mysteries, and so on; all have a distinct culture and power. What we must come to experientially know is the different facets of prayer within our mandate; we must also engage in all prayer. Thus, in the upcoming chapters we will venture into some of the facets of prayer so that we can engage more holistically the concept of "all prayer." I pray that the Father of Glory grant you the spirit of understanding and revelation. In Jesus' Name.

CHAPTER 7

Intercessory Prayer

Our Position in Prayer

Previously, I defined what it is to intercede; we have covered in some depth how Christ is the Chief of Intercession and also touched on how we are joined directly with His intercession and how we are called to do the same. If you would like to refresh yourself in those insights, please return to the chapter entitled, "The Preeminence of Christ in Prayer."

In this chapter, I would like to cover what our function in intercession is before entering into the heart of the matter. Again, the term "intercession," through the Latin root, *intercedere*, is a verb meaning, "To go between." It is the action of a mediator—to intervene—to come between so as to prevent or alter a result or course of events. As Scripture tells us in 2 Corinthians 5:18-21:

> *All this is from God, who through Christ reconciled us to himself and gave us the ministry of reconciliation; that is, in Christ God was reconciling the world to himself, not counting their trespasses against them, and entrusting to us the message of reconciliation. Therefore, we are ambassadors for Christ, God making his appeal through us. We implore you on behalf of Christ, be reconciled to God. For our sake he made him to be sin who knew no sin, so that in him we might become the righteousness of God.*

Therefore, since Christ is the Chief Intercessor, we, as partakers of ministry, are an extension of Christ's finished work of intercession. Scripture reveals that Jesus is the Head and we are His body; we know that the head is not the extension of the body, but the body is the extension of the head. In this image, the Holy Spirit is the neck, which tells the body where to go through His connection to the Head, which is Christ. For that reason, our intercession means we are receiving from heaven and partnering with Jesus' desires for the earth. Prayer is the currency that brings forth change. When we intercede, we are yoking ourselves with Christ by the Spirit of God before the omnipotent Father. Though Christ intercedes, God is looking for us to yoke ourselves to Him as His extension to bring forth His finished work in the earth.

When we receive and partake of the New Covenant of Christ by the Holy Spirit, we are immediately seated with Him in heavenly places. As Scripture tells us in Ephesians 2:4-7:

But God, being rich in mercy, because of the great love with which he loved us, even when we were dead in our trespasses, made us alive together with Christ—by grace you have been saved—and raised us up with him and seated us with him in the heavenly places in Christ Jesus, so that in the coming ages he might show the immeasurable riches of his grace in kindness toward us in Christ Jesus.

Understand that to be positioned beside Christ is not a matter of physical location, but it is a decree of authority. Jesus has all authority at the right hand of God, and as an extension of Him, we share in that privilege, even as we walk this earth. Our authority does not flow from our positions or function on the earth, but our position with Christ in the heavens. We are seen in light of the authority of Christ, which is why Jesus, at our commissioning, states:

Go into all the world and proclaim the gospel to the whole creation. Whoever believes and is baptized will be saved, but whoever does not believe will be condemned. And these signs will accompany those who believe: in my name they will cast out demons; they will speak in new tongues; they will pick up serpents with their hands; and if they drink any deadly poison, it will not hurt them; they will lay their hands on the sick, and they will recover. (Mark 16:15-18)

The power to do these things comes from being an extension of Jesus Christ. Thus, we can do all the things that He has commanded us, for we have been granted the authority through Him:

All authority in heaven and on earth has been given to me. Go therefore and make disciples of all nations, baptizing them in the name of the Father and of the Son and of the Holy Spirit, teaching them to observe all that I have commanded you. And behold, I am with you always, to the end of the age. (Matthew 28:18-20)

As this is spiritual knowledge, please do not attempt to understand by the manner of the flesh and an un-renewed mind. Allow the Holy Spirit to root you in the knowledge of God and thrust you into operating in the manner of our position in heaven. Demons flee not because we say, "In the name of Jesus," but because our words are backed by the power of heaven; therefore, we can say, "Demon, flee," and it does. We can say, "Be healed!" and the sick are made whole; for Ephesians 2:7 also tells us that we are positioned with Christ so that God can show the "immeasurable riches of his grace." So as we move on to share in the heart of intercession, let us be aware that ours is the extension of Christ's finished work and the release of what He has inherited by His intercession into the earth.

Before we continue, I implore you to remember that the reason we are expounding on "the heart" more is because intercession is not words; it is the posture and intent of our hearts. We can know our hearts in the Lord, because our prayers reflect them. If our prayers are more about wealth, we know our hearts are set on wealth. Whatever we are dedicated to praying for is where we find the heart of our intercession. So when we come to the intercession of the Church, Scripture shows us specifically three "hearts" that we are to dedicate and intercede before the Lord with: our heart for the Lord, our heart for the Church, and our heart for the world. If you were made a child of God, believing in the cross and that Jesus is the resurrected Lord and Savior, you are called to this ministry of intercession, individually and corporately by the Holy Spirit.

With that said, let us go forward into the three hearts of intercession and break into the insights that may transform our lives. I pray that the power of the Holy Spirit be upon you and increases your capacity to receive every word in its truth. Also, I pray for His revelatory presence to propel you into the hearts and ministry of intercession. In Jesus's Name.

The Hearts of Intercession

1. Our Heart for the Lord

Within intercession, the posture of our hearts must be toward the Lord. The Lord does not have the capacity to not consume what is around Him, for He is all-consuming. When you enter into a relationship with Him, He will consume your mind, your heart, and your desires. When I began dedicating myself to intercession, I found that many times it was through conversation with the Holy Spirit that my heart could feel His, and I knew exactly what to pray for. Intercession is born from a place of oneness with the Lord. We will understand His power and what consumes His heart as we draw closer.

Intercession with the Lord is like first looking at the ocean afar; the closer you get, the further you realize its magnitude! So it is with the heartbeat of God. Afar off you can adore its beauty, but the extent you are consumed depends on your closeness.

Intercession is born in a place of oneness with the Lord. Jeremiah the prophet understood this; he is known as the "weeping prophet," and I believe this means he was close to the heart of a weeping God. The heart of Israel was corrupt, and the Lord's heart was broken. Similarly, Jeremiah states, "My heart is broken within me; all my bones shake; I am like a drunken man, like a man overcome by wine, because of the Lord and because of his holy words" (Jeremiah 23:9). Notice that he says his heart's condition is not just because of the condition of the land, but because of the Lord and His holy words. When we enter into true friendship with the Lord, He will share with us the deep secrets of His heart. Like any friend, He will share with us what burdens Him and what makes Him joyful; what pleases Him, and what He despises. You will become one with Him. Jeremiah, with the heart of God near his own, states, "If I say, 'I will not mention him, or speak any more in his name,' there is in my heart as it were a burning fire shut up in my bones, and I am weary with holding it in, and I cannot" (Jeremiah 20:9). Even when he tried to stop speaking the word of the Lord to Israel, his heart could not handle it, and it drove him to the place of prayer and intercession.

Jeremiah seemed to complain, but I believe it was deeper than complaint. Due to the blindness of the people's hearts and God's sorrow because of them, he was stuck in a place of intercession; Jeremiah could do nothing but mourn as an intercessor for Israel.

Because intercession is born in the place of oneness with the Lord, the intercessor knows the heart of the Lord through the Spirit of God, and from that point knows exactly what to intercede for. If your intercession is born out of flesh and not by the heart of the Spirit, you are strictly mistaken of your prayers effectiveness. Intercessors who spend time with the Lord see like Him. Because they share His heart, His will, and His burden, they will see, hear, and feel what He feels. So-called "intercessors" who are more concerned about what they desire to see than the desires of the Lord's heart are deceiving themselves into believing that they are a part of Christ's ministry of intercession; we should not forget that it is Christ's ministry, and we are but partakers in it. As said in a previous chapter, Jesus said, "Come to me, all who labor and are heavy laden, and I will give you rest. Take my yoke upon you, and learn from me" (Matthew 11:28). Intercession is the yoke of the Lord, and we will never walk with Him unless we learn from Him. The Spirit of God is here to reveal this to us!

Intercession is born in the place of oneness with the Lord. Intercessors meet with God. If we understand this, humility and lowliness will guard our hearts from anything less than the heart of God.

2. Our Heart for the Church

The Word of God commissions us to intercede for each other in the body of Christ. Paul opened many of his epistles with prayers for his readers and asked at the benediction for his readers to pray for him. He exemplified the words of Ephesians 6:18: "praying at all times in the Spirit, with all prayer and supplication. To that end, keep alert with all perseverance, making supplication for all the saints." Supplication means, "To earnestly intercede for."

Intercessors pave the way for deliverance, and the Lord has commanded us to pray for one another, to cover and admonish one another in love. What must it look like to pray for everything else other than your brother in the Lord who is struggling with sin? You are your brother's keeper, and your prayer for them must come from a heart for them. As 1 John 4:20-21 states:

> If anyone says, "I love God," and hates his brother, he is a liar; for he who does not love his brother whom he has seen cannot love God whom he has not seen. And this commandment we have from him: whoever loves God must also love his brother.

If intercession is born from oneness with the Lord, the condition, affairs, and direction of our brothers and sisters in the Lord will fill our hearts.

I have seen many over-spiritual intercessors that will pray for you seemingly for their own benefit and not out of love for you. We as intercessors cannot become so shallow that we forget to pray for one another out of God's consuming love. For example, as I began to yield myself more and more to being in the place of intercession with the Lord, I would be with my family in Christ and mourn silently within myself because I could feel the love of God for them. It was as if I could see the conditions of their lives, and it would thrust me back into the place of intercession.

Intercession for the saints must come out of love. Love is what propelled Jesus to the cross, and it is love that propels Him to pray for us today. A part of our lives as believers is to be concerned with the growth, condition, and situation of our brothers. This goes beyond their prayer requests. I am not talking about being nosey and meddling; I am talking about sincere concern and love for one another in our pursuit of the Lord. Our hearts for one another should propel us to pray rather than gossip. You cannot hate someone you sincerely pray for. It is better to say nothing than to promise to pray for someone and proceed not to. The Lord confronted me on this issue; the Spirit was very saddened and warned me to never do it again. To this day, that conviction lies deep within, and I have come to understand that when someone asks me to pray for them, it is a invitation to partner with Christ and hear His heart concerning them.

I believe if we begin to sincerely pray for one another in the body of Christ, we will see her arise in the world and supernaturally infiltrate every sphere of culture in the power of the Spirit and filled with the love of the Lord.

3. Our Heart for the World

Lastly for this subtopic, intercession is the hidden sickle of harvesting the world. As Corey Russell wrote, "The Church is awakening to the truth that Jesus is not only the great Evangelist; He is also the eternal Intercessor. The Intercessor is leading the missions movement, and the Evangelist is leading the prayer and worship movement" (194-195). Jesus, the Great Evangelist, declared a call to reap the harvest as it records in Matthew 9:35-38:

> *And Jesus went throughout all the cities and villages, teaching in their synagogues and proclaiming the gospel of the kingdom and healing every disease and every affliction. When he saw the crowds, he had compassion for them, because they were harassed and helpless, like sheep without a shepherd. Then he said to his disciples, "The harvest is plentiful, but the laborers are few; therefore pray earnestly to the Lord of the harvest to send out laborers into his harvest."*

Before we discuss what intercession for the world looks like, I want to make sure that we all understand that we are called to pray and go into the harvest. What we see in America is the neglect of the harvest and a push for comfort in the four walls of the Church. True, we are called to pray; however, Jesus also called us to embrace the world with His love. We have neglected the destitute and the spiritually dead as we enjoy "church," which has become a building of paraplegic beds (we call them pews), resulting in the obesity of the Church and the deaths of many souls who do not know the love of God. Since this book is not about evangelism, let us see how our heart for the world matters in our intercession.

Our intercession is used to bear sinners into the kingdom of God. Isaiah 66:8 states: "Who has heard such a thing? Who has seen such things? Shall a land be born in one day? Shall a nation be brought forth in one moment? For as soon as Zion was in labor she brought forth her children" (ESV). We understand by faith and by interpretation that Isaiah was prophetically speaking of the Church. He says that as soon as Zion (the Church) was in labor (prayer), she would bring forth her children (converts).

There is a word used mostly in the OT called "travail"; this term is used in the book of the prophets and is associated with the anguish of childbirth, or "painful or laborious effort." Jesus travailed for the world on the cross. In Isaiah 53:11, it states: "He shall see of the travail of his soul, and shall be satisfied: by his knowledge shall my righteous servant justify many; for he shall bear their iniquities" (KJV).

The Word of God never says that Jesus stopped praying for the world and now intercedes only on our behalf. We in the body of Christ are the result of Jesus' travail for the world, and as we are partakers of such ministry, our hearts should be filled with compassion for the same. Jesus was led by compassion and charged the disciples to pray for the harvest to be reaped by laborers. As said in possibly the most widely-known Scripture:

> For God so loved the world, that he gave his only Son, that whoever believes in him should not perish but have eternal life. For God did not send his Son into the world to condemn the world, but in order that the world might be saved through him. (John 3:16-17)

So, beloved, I pray that the compassion of the Lord fills your heart for the drunkard, the depressed, the prostitute, the murderer, the rapist, and the pedophile. In this wise, you may, yoked with Christ, partake of bringing them into the kingdom. We are called to not love the things of the world, but we are called to the love its people. I remember when the Lord burdened my heart for those who have given themselves over to an alternative lifestyle. I saw the darkness, oppression, and dominion of the kingdom of deception. I could see the people from afar, and my heart began to mourn for their salvation. I mourned for prisoners, asking the Lord to encounter them. I interceded for teens who are lost and aimless, who turn to gangs and defilement. I mourned for the sisters who give themselves to any man who calls them beautiful. I mourned for the salvation of the homeless and destitute. I remember the Lord awakening me to pray for drunk drivers; there, I stepped into a place of God's heart that was so weighty that I almost could not handle it. I would receive dreams and visions of lost loved ones and begin to call on the Lord to break into their lives and save their hearts. I was filled with nothing but love for the world.

Moved with compassion, we must begin to pray that the Lord will strengthen and launch the laborers into the harvest—the nations of this world. I know without a shadow of a doubt that we are on the dawn of the greatest harvest history has ever seen, and it shall be born through the intercession of the sons and daughters of God and seen as a result of them finally obeying the command to go into all the earth and make disciples of all nations. This kind of intercession is coupled with our labor in the harvest. Having one without the other is like have a hand without feet. Intercession is the birthing canal, but our acts of compassion and love are the reapers.

Burdens, Assignments, and Mysteries

"Can I recommend you to the Lord for prayer?" said my friend. I immediately answered with a resounding, "Yes!" When engaging the intercessory world, the spiritual culture is filled with burdens, assignments, and mysteries. My friend's question started an amazing journey of thought, as the Lord revealed to me that even though the entire body of Christ is responsible to act in the ministry of intercession, not everyone is called to intercede for the same thing.

The Lord brought me to a few years back. On a particular day, as I was trying to pray, I fell asleep. As I slept, I dreamt of standing on a huge calendar, in the month of July. The dates of the 12th, 13th and 14th were highlighted below me. The Lord then said to me, "Walk from the 12th to the 14th." When I began to walk toward the 14th, I began to physically decline. Then the Lord said, "Fast and pray for Nigeria for the next three days." Immediately, I woke and began this journey of prayer. To this day, many parts of that assignment from the Lord were and still are a mystery to me. I watched the news specifically for them as I prayed for their economy, government, and president. I even remember that as I interceded, I had a vision of myself standing in the presidential office, praying over the presidential table and chair. I could see the papers on the desk of financial status and plans asking the Lord to give them wisdom and free them from any compromised way. I prayed by the help of the Holy Spirit's governance for those three days, and when the 14th of July came, the burden and unction to pray for them ceased.

To this day, I love Nigeria and believe they are permanently in my heart, for I will never forget how I felt their need deeply within my heart. That is only an example of what I mean by burdens, assignments, and mysteries, which I will explain next:

1. *Burdens*

The term "burden" means a load, especially a heavy one. When something is a burden, it troubles us and weighs upon us. So it is in intercession. Burdens can be various conditions, situations, and events that vex your heart, thrusting you into a place of prayer. In the prayer movement today, the Lord is burdening many to arise in prayer for social justice. We hear many voices crying out for moral resurgence, crying out to the Lord for reformation, wailing for help to come for abortion and sex-trafficking victims. This is what you call a burden. It is a heavy load within your spirit that propels you to the place of intercession, weeping before the Lord.

I can recall when the Lord released a burden on my heart for the rebuilding of Church walls. As I repeated the same phrase, "God, rebuild your temple," I began to weep on my side on the floor. I could feel my insides get crushed by the burden in my spirit. I believe this is what Jeremiah was feeling when He said, "My heart is broken within me; all my bones shake; I am like a drunken man, like a man overcome by wine, because of the Lord and because of his holy words" (Jeremiah 23:9). Burdens are a consequence of our nearness to God and His trust in us. I believe that when the Lord called Jeremiah and saw his obedience and humility, He knew He could trust him with the burdens of His heart for Israel. When the Lord burdens you with something, take it not lightly, for the Lord has entrusted a disturbance of His Spirit to you. I weep for the nations, I weep for the Church, and I weep for my generation. It is not because of how "bad" it is; it is because the Lord has entrusted me with that burden.

2. Assignments

Now, assignments are different from burdens. However, if you carry them long enough, they might become so. The Oxford Dictionary explains the term assignment to mean, "A task or piece of work assigned to someone as part of a job or course of study." ("Assignment" def. 5). Assignments are tasks that the Lord has called and chosen someone to accomplish. For instance, Jonah the prophet was called to an assignment without a burden, but he ran from his assignment, which became a burden the further he went. This landed him in the belly of a fish for three days, which finally propelled him to the place of intercession and brought him right where he was supposed to be in the first place. Paul had a burden for the Jews even though he was called and assigned to the Gentiles. It was when the Jews rejected and persecuted him that he left for his assignment to the Gentiles. Assignments are the consequence of your availability and simply require your obedience. For example, Joseph of the OT did not have a burden for Egypt but for Israel, but the Lord assigned him as prime-minister of Egypt for the fulfillment of his burden for Israel.

3. Mysteries

Mysteries are just that: mysteries. The Lord has equipped us to pray out mysteries that even our minds cannot understand. As stated in 1 Corinthians 14:2, 13-15:

> For one who speaks in a tongue speaks not to men but to God; for no one understands him, but he utters mysteries in the Spirit. Therefore, one who speaks in a tongue should pray that he may interpret. For if I pray in a tongue, my spirit prays but my mind is unfruitful. What am I to do? I will pray with my spirit, but I will pray with my mind also; I will sing praise with my spirit, but I will sing with my mind also.

Specifically dealing with mysteries, this passage shows us that the Lord equips and has empowered our spirits by the Holy Spirit to speak in an encrypted language just to communicate with Him. I do not wish to argue this concept, so I recommend you read Corey Russell's book, *The Glory Within*, which is dedicated to the topic of tongues, and *The Holy Spirit: An Introduction* by John Bevere, who also expounds on the mystery of tongues. I again warn you not the attempt to understand spiritual things with the un-renewed thinking of the flesh. Allow the Holy Spirit to do whatever He wills and release all of the gifts that Scripture tells us He has for us.

To engage with the Lord in the language of mysteries is to use this gift in private prayer. Paul, who tells us that the Lord charged Him to reveal the mysteries of the kingdom, says, "I thank God that I speak in tongues more than all of you" (1 Corinthians 14:18). The man who revealed many mysteries also avidly prayed in tongues. I believe there must be some correlation. Tongues releases a sense of humility to our hearts and allows us to venture deeper with the Lord, spirit to Spirit. The number one reason that I believe many are against speaking in tongues is the issue of pride. We are unwilling to give up the control of our intellect to engage with the Lord on a solely humble and deeply spiritual place. There were times that the Lord called me to prayer, and all I could do by the leadership of the Holy Spirit was speak in the language of mysteries. I would set my mind on the Lord, and as I prayed in my private spiritual language, there would seemingly bubble in my heart words that I understood, and then I would pray them out. This is what Paul meant by praying with the spirit and also with understanding (1 Corinthians 14:15). As I continued, I would sense the affirmation of the Holy Spirit and keep going. Not everyone has this gift, but I believe it is available to all by faith. This gift is for the edification of yourself within prayer and if with public demonstration and interpretation it also edifies the body of Christ (1 Corinthians 14:2, 4-5, 13).

These three facets are interlaced. Many times we will receive a burden or an assignment as we pray in mysteries (tongues), or pray in mysteries because we do not intellectually understand how to pray on a particular assignment, or our burden is so deep that it is the assignment of our lives, and we can only pray with our spirits in the language of mysteries. Either way, when we open ourselves up to the world of true intercession, all of these different dimensions will begin to open to us, and we will begin to engage with the Lord in many ways as the Spirit leads.

The spiritual gifts are ours to exercise by the Spirit, and God is faithful to those who humble themselves and try in faith His word. It is sure, and its sayings are true and ever current. Paul even states in 1 Corinthians 12:1, 4-6:

> *Now concerning spiritual gifts, brothers, I do not want you to be uninformed...Now there are varieties of gifts, but the same Spirit; and there are varieties of service, but the same Lord; and there are varieties of activities, but it is the same God who empowers them all in everyone.*

I implore you to receive and not neglect spiritual things. There are many teachings, especially about tongues, but I implore you to favor the Word of God as you pursue the Lord in your relationship with the Holy Spirit.

Recap

The authority and power of intercession comes from our position with the Lord. Possessing the heart of intercession is more valuable than our activity; therefore, the "hearts" of intercession are our heart for the Lord, our heart for the Church, and our heart for the world. When we begin to engage the world of intercession, we receive many dimensional understandings and engage with the Lord in different facets of prayer such as burdens, assignments and mysteries.

I pray the Lord empowers you to enter into all that is written in this chapter and that you holistically engage with Him in intercession. I pray the eyes of your heart be enlightened and you receive the gifts of the Spirit to propel you into a deeper place of partnering with the Lord, even in prayer. In Jesus' Name. Can you be recommended for prayer?

CHAPTER 8

Corporate Intercession

The Spirit of Gathering

The fervency of corporate intercession has seemingly dwindled in today's Church, and I believe this is because we have yet to realize the differences between corporate and private intercession. We see this when people run away from corporate prayer meetings because of a lack of understanding. The problem is that they are trying to enjoy intimacy with the Lord as a friend, when the purpose of the meeting is to seek audience with God as King.

Scripture continually charges us to gather with each other in atmospheres and dimensions of intercession. The problem many times with the believers who are hindered in corporate gatherings of prayer is that they lack the spirit of gathering. The spirit of gathering is not another name for the Holy Spirit or an angel. It is likened to the unity of a group with the same interest and mindset. Thus, I want to dedicate this chapter to specifically expound on the importance, culture and difference of corporate intercession.

1. The Importance

I believe the first order of business when it comes to corporate prayer is to understand its importance, because if we embrace its importance, we can soberly exercise its purpose and see great manifestations of God answering prayer. The Lord commanded the prophet Joel to cry out to Israel, saying:

> *Consecrate a fast; call a solemn assembly. Gather the elders and all the inhabitants of the land to the house of the Lord your God, and cry out to the Lord.* (Joel 1:14).

The urgency of this verse and the weight of its call were heavy on Joel. The Lord was calling not just for individual intercession behind closed doors, but for something far bigger; He told His prophet to cry out for all of Israel to gather and cry out for their land. This call was sent for the purpose of showing mercy to the people as they gathered together with the same heart toward God.

When we gather together as one people with the same heart and focus before the Lord, it is to meet with Him for the sake of invoking His power and merciful will in our time. Scripture and prophecy speak to the people of God:

> *Gather to me my faithful ones, who made a covenant with me by sacrifice! The heavens declare his righteousness, for God himself is judge!* (Psalm 50:5-6)

When we gather as believers, we are meeting to hear the judgments of God according to our intercession. The gathering is not just for us to pray in the name of Jesus but to be gathered for the same purpose in same heart in prayer, for as Jesus said in Matthew 18:20, "For where two or three are gathered in my name, there am I among them." We must be "gathered" in His name, not just gathered to speak it. When we are "gathered" in His name, we incite a meeting with the King. God shows this when He dealt with Israel in the wilderness:

> *Make them known to your children and your children's children—how on the day that you stood before the Lord your God at Horeb, the Lord said to me, "Gather the people to me, that I may let them hear my words, so that they may learn to fear me all the days that they live on the earth, and that they may teach their children so." And you came near and stood at the foot of the mountain, while the mountain burned with fire to the heart of heaven, wrapped in darkness, cloud, and gloom. Then the Lord spoke to you out of the midst of the fire. You heard the sound of words, but saw no form; there was only a voice. And he declared to you his covenant.* (Deuteronomy 4:9-13)

In that time, the people of God gathered before Him, and He did not speak only through His prophets, but He desired to open the heavens and speak with them face-to-face. He desires the same for us in modern times; for a personal example, during my studies at Oral Roberts University, up to 500 students gathered every Friday night and prayed earnestly for God to release spiritual resurgence on our campus. The Lord spoke to us many times concerning His judgment of our campus, and we knew how to continue to pray into those heavenly verdicts, that the Lord would release the promised move of His Spirit. We spoke about the Lord giving to us the authority to declare the heavenly legalities on the earth and subduing the kingdom of darkness for the advancement of the Gospel, for again, as Jesus says in Matthew 18:18, "Truly, I say to you, whatever you bind on earth shall be bound in heaven, and whatever you loose on earth shall be loosed in heaven."

The fact of the matter is that God loves and blesses unity. There is a special grace when we come together, because we could accomplish together in a day what could have taken generations as an individualistic assignment. For again, as Isaiah 66:8 states, "Who has heard such a thing? Who has seen such things? Shall a land be born in one day? Shall a nation be brought forth in one moment? For as soon as Zion was in labor she brought forth her children." As soon as we gather ourselves in the labor of intercession, we can lead nations toward salvation and the kingdom of God.

2. *The Culture*

Every believer who has received the Holy Spirit has also received spiritual gifts and blessings. Scripture states:

> *For by the grace given to me I say to everyone among you not to think of himself more highly than he ought to think, but to think with sober judgment, each according to the measure of faith that God has assigned. For as in one body we have many members, and the members do not all have the same function, so we, though many, are one body in Christ, and individually members one of another. Having gifts that differ according to the grace given to us, let us use them: if prophecy, in proportion to our faith; if service, in our serving; the one who teaches, in his teaching; the one who exhorts, in his exhortation; the one who contributes, in generosity; the one who leads, with zeal; the one who does acts of mercy, with cheerfulness.* (Romans 12:3-8)

God has given each of us gifts to be exercised in faith. We might not have the same gifts, but we are part of a body. Since our gifts differ "according to the grace given to us," we operate in the grace we receive. For instance, you may have the grace to write books; thus, you operate in that grace. The Lord may have blessed you financially; thus, you are charged to operate according to the grace of generosity. For our benefit, the Scripture explains the diverse functions and gifts:

> *Now there are varieties of gifts, but the same Spirit; and there are varieties of service, but the same Lord; and there are varieties of activities, but it is the same God who empowers them all in everyone. To each is given the manifestation of the Spirit for the common good. For to one is given through the Spirit the utterance of wisdom, and to another the utterance of knowledge according to the same Spirit, to another faith by the same Spirit, to another gifts of healing by the one Spirit, to another the working of miracles, to another prophecy, to another the ability to distinguish between spirits, to another various kinds of tongues, to another the interpretation of tongues. All these are empowered by one and the same Spirit, who apportions to each one individually as he wills.* (1 Corinthians 12:4-11)

Within this passage, we are enlightened to what the culture of our gatherings should be as the body of Christ.

In corporate intercession, there are different functions and gifts that are utilized by the Spirit with an individual. As we intercede together, we have the benefit of various abilities that help us to accomplish more than we could ever do with our own manifestation of the Spirit. For example, you may be the eyes in the body of Christ and are able to see the plans of the Lord; another may be the ear, able to hear the counsel of the Lord in the Spirit. If you just see a vision and do not have the counsel or interpretation, you only know in part what the Lord might do, but if the abilities are put together in prayer, the Lord will use them to give a more holistic understanding of His plans and power. Thus, there is an assurance that we, graced with different functions, can all play a part in receiving complete revelations from the Lord in our gatherings.

The culture of corporate intercession requires appreciation, discernment and harmony. When the Lord calls us together we are all a vital part of Him revealing His will and judgments to us. Thus, we must be continually empowered and led by the Holy Spirit to assure that we are incorporating all of the different functions of the body.

3. The Difference

We see that without each other, we are not receiving the total revelation. If we individually attempt to override the different functions of corporate intercession—either in a mindset of pride or a misunderstanding of what harmony requires and releases—it only causes confusion. Paul revisits this issue of harmony in the Church, writing:

> *What then, brothers? When you come together, each one has a hymn, a lesson, a revelation, a tongue, or an interpretation. Let all things be done for building up. If any speak in a tongue, let there be only two or at most three, and each in turn, and let someone interpret. But if there is no one to interpret, let each of them keep silent in church and speak to himself and to God. Let two or three prophets speak, and let the others weigh what is said. If a revelation is made to another sitting there, let the first be silent. For you can all prophesy one by one, so that all may learn and all be encouraged, and the spirits of prophets are subject to prophets. For God is not a God of confusion but of peace.* (1 Corinthians 14:26-33)

Paul is telling the reader to let everyone accomplish their allotted task when they come together, so that the group is built up and edified; one may have a vision, and another may have a revelation of the same thing; when we come together, especially in prayer, we must, by the leading of the Holy Spirit, allow each other to share according to our specific grace, that all may learn and be edified in the knowledge of the Holy One. We must not do this in a chaotic or flippant way, but in a sober-minded and humble manner, that the Lord may be the focus and His revelation the spotlight. Corporate intercession requires prophetic insights, yet when we operate in a prideful and pushy manner it only causes confusion and disrupts the peace. Peace is not necessarily quietness, but harmony.

Corporate intercession is needed, and we need everyone, every manifestation of the Holy Spirit, in every gift. We cannot come to a corporate gathering to engage with the Lord intimately as if we are not around one another. There is no such things as "doing your own thing" in an assembly setting. Our gatherings are meant to edify and encourage each other as we receive from the Lord together.

Going back to my campus example, I remember a time when we gathered as fellow students to pray for revival on our campus. Many left because they were trying to do their own thing, and the corporate setting was disturbing them. In actuality, they were disturbing the corporate setting because they were not joining in one accord. The Holy Spirit did not have an outbreak when the disciples prayed alone, but when 120 of them gathered and prayed, the Holy Spirit broke in with signs and wonders, and that day 3,000 people were added to the Church (Acts 2:41). In this place of corporate intercession, the Lord released His promises to them. Yes, the disciples were all touched individually and intimately impacted, but there, in a place of one accord with one another, they all sought the same promise the Lord revealed to them. We must do the same today.

The Importance of Leadership

A sense of order in corporate prayer is needed to maintain the peace of God, and to maintain this, the Holy Spirit will always raise a group of leaders to ensure that the focus of the gathering is kept. Today, a spirit of rebellion captures the hearts of many because they want to do their own thing and are not permitted to lead; therefore, we have many different pockets of intercessory gatherings born from offense and rebellion. For as Scripture says:

> *Behold, how good and pleasant it is when brothers dwell in unity! It is like the precious oil on the head, running down on the beard, on the beard of Aaron, running down on the collar of his robes! It is like the dew of Hermon, which falls on the mountains of Zion! For there the Lord has commanded the blessing, life forevermore.* (Psalm 133:1-3)

At the end, God shows that where there is unity amongst the brothers, there is blessing and life. Leaders are chosen by the Lord to oversee this unity and to make sure that the brothers are in one accord. Many of these leaders operate in a prophetic anointing and must be highly sensitive to the leading of the Holy Spirit. Without leadership, the Church would not have survived, for without all the parts working together, she would have fallen into chaos; Ephesians 4:11-14 shows how each member has a purpose and role:

> *And he gave the apostles, the prophets, the evangelists, the shepherds and teachers, to equip the saints for the work of ministry, for building up the body of Christ, until we all attain to the unity of the faith and of the knowledge of the Son of God, to mature manhood, to the measure of the stature of the fullness of Christ, so that we may no longer be children, tossed to and fro by the waves and carried about by every wind of doctrine, by human cunning, by craftiness in deceitful schemes.*

These foundational gifts are needed to ensure that the body of Christ is equipped for the work of the ministry of the Holy Spirit, to build up the Church in unity and in the knowledge of Christ.

The importance of leadership submitted to the lordship of the Holy Spirit is weighty; only those who appreciate the order will garner its benefit. Most of the assemblies in the OT were led by the prophets, kings, and priests under the lordship of the Spirit or under a specific cause such as repentance or deliverance from enemies. The Lord once spoke to me and said, "I have not given you kings but shepherds; I have not given you rulers according to their will but servants according to mine." Leaders are servant—an extension of the Lord's shepherding staff; thus, we must appreciate their function and operate under the lordship of the Spirit, not defying the leadership He set in place. And leaders must serve the people of God with humble hearts, expecting the Lord to speak through the congregation as much as He would speak to them.

Forsake not the functions of the assembly, but appreciate and permit them with discernment for the cause of harmony, edification, encouragement, exhortation, and the building up and common good of all. When we pray, let us be of one accord in heart and mind, focused in prayer on the same thing, that we open the heavens and meet with God together.

Recap

Corporate intercession occurs so the body of Christ will assemble in unity to meet with and hear from the Lord. We are charged by Scripture to come together because God loves and empowers us when we are in one accord. We must remember the importance of assembling together in obedience to the Word of God and His Spirit. We must remember the culture of gatherings so that we do not become prideful or ignorantly attempt to do our "own thing"; instead, we will do all things for the good of each other.

We all have different functions, abilities and graces that together will result in a more holistic revelation of God's judgments, counsel and will. Leaders are to operate under the lordship and unction of the Holy Spirit, making sure that the entire assembly is in one accord and disperses without strife: edified, encouraged, and built up in the knowledge of the Lord. We must not allow the spirit of rebellion and offense to rob us from our unity and the power we receive from being together. All in all, we need leadership to assure that our gatherings are conducted in order and harmony.

I pray you will receive the knowledge in this chapter and that the Holy Spirit will reveal even more. I pray that as you assemble with the people of God, your contribution will be purely of and from the Holy Spirit as he empowers you to edify your local assembly. In Jesus' Name.

CHAPTER 9

Prayer and...

Prayer and Fasting

This chapter is dedicated to speaking about three main spiritual practices namely, fasting, worship, and prophecy, which increase our knowledge of the Lord and empower us to go deeper into all that prayer is.

Our first staple is prayer and fasting. According to the Oxford Dictionary, "fasting" means "to abstain from food." ("Fasting" def. 6). Today, many spiritual infants in the body of Christ do not understand its purpose, believing that it is merely an extra practice. Jesus does not state, "*If* you fast," but "WHEN you fast," implying that fasting is not optional.

> *And when you fast, do not look gloomy like the hypocrites, for they disfigure their faces that their fasting may be seen by others. Truly, I say to you, they have received their reward.* (Matthew 6:16)

Here is how we should fast: firstly, fasting should be a consistent private practice in our walk of faith. We are to do it in private to protect ourselves from operating in pride, hypocrisy and self-righteousness, for as Jesus said:

> *But when you fast, anoint your head and wash your face, that your fasting may not be seen by others but by your Father who is in secret. And your Father who sees in secret will reward you.* (Matthew 6:17-18)

Secondly, during the fast, we must set our hearts toward the Father; should we do so, He will reward us. Now, when we fast, we are not doing it to earn anything. If we could gain through human works, Jesus would not have needed to die on the cross. Instead, we fast to receive freely from the Lord by voluntarily abstaining from earthly things for heavenly things. For example, when Jesus was fasting for 40 days and nights, the devil tried to convince Him to turn stone into bread, tempting Him with the physical hunger of His mortal body. Jesus rebuked him, saying, "It is written, 'Man shall not live by bread alone, but by every word that comes from the mouth of God'" (Matthew 4:4). His words reveal that He was embracing His physical weakness for reasons of the spirit. This struggle is one that all who fast must face.

Prayer without a tenderized heart leaves us blinded to the beauty of God, and fasting is what softens the hard areas. It is a tool to enlighten us to what we really need and creates spiritual hunger. Through it, we find out just how much we eat away our spiritual hunger through earthly and worldly desires. We learn how intense our pursuit of God truly is, and we see how diligent we really are in setting the plate down and turning the prime-time television off to cry out to God. Fasting is a louder declaration of inner spiritual hunger than vocalized prayer alone can ever be, and abstaining from something is an action more potent than empty words; a man who spends time with the Lord instead of continuing to watch ESPN is declaring from his heart that he desires a relationship with God more than he wants to satisfy his fleshly desires. Jesus in Matthew 5:6 says, "Blessed are those who hunger and thirst for righteousness, for they shall be satisfied." This statement is perfectly relatable to fasting, because when we fast, we are hungering and thirsting for something that food and entertainment cannot give us, for we are opening ourselves to be filled with the rewards of the Father.

Fasting is embracing the weakness of our flesh and asking God for His supernatural power. When we fast, we are declaring to God that no earthly thing or idea can accomplish what our hearts need; He is our only option. Like a mother troubled for the sake of her wayward child, it is hard for her to take pleasure in anything else because her mourning and desire has overtaken her hunger for anything else. Likewise, fasting helps us to remember our consistent need for God's presence and power in our lives.

Isaiah 58:3 states, "'Why have we fasted, and you see it not? Why have we humbled ourselves, and you take no knowledge of it?' Behold, in the day of your fast you seek your own pleasure." The question in the beginning of this verse is from the people of Israel, who are asking God why He has not rewarded their fasting and praying. What God's response reveals is that when we fast and allow our spiritual hunger to override the desires of our flesh, our spiritual hunger should conform to the desires of God. As Romans 8:5 says, "For those who live according to the flesh set their minds on the things of the flesh, but those who live according to the Spirit set their minds on the things of the Spirit."

God reprimanded the people of Israel because they sought their own pleasure, not the Lord's. "Fasting like yours this day will not make your voice to be heard on high," He said to them (Isaiah 58:4). He says this because they called out to Him as if they were hungering for His desires, when in actuality they we hungering for their own. When we abstain from earthly desires by fasting, it is to embrace a tender spirit for the things of God's heart. God reveals the desires of His heart to the people of Israel in Isaiah 58:6-9:

> *Is not this the fast that I choose: to loose the bonds of wickedness, to undo the straps of the yoke, to let the oppressed go free, and to break every yoke? Is it not to share your bread with the hungry and bring the homeless poor into your house; when you see the naked, to cover him, and not to hide yourself from your own flesh? Then shall your light break forth like the dawn, and your healing shall spring up speedily; your righteousness shall go before you; the glory of the Lord shall be your rear guard. Then you shall call, and the Lord will answer; you shall cry, and he will say, "Here I am."*

Let us break these verses down:

1. *To loose the bonds of wickedness, to undo the straps of the yoke, to let the oppressed go free, and to break every yoke?*

   The Lord begins with His desire for wickedness, bondage, oppression, and every sinful weight to be lifted off of our lives; as Galatians 5:1 says, "For freedom Christ has set us free; stand firm therefore, and do not submit again to a yoke of slavery." The Lord wants to free us from all habitual sins, shame, guilt, and oppressive darkness. Thus, when we fast, let us set our hearts to see this become a reality in our lives and in the lives of others. The Lord may burden you to fast and pray for a certain person who is bound by darkness and depression (demonic forms of oppression), and by your obedience to fast and pray, the Lord would break in and save them. When the disciples could not cast out a certain evil spirit oppressing a young boy, the Lord taught them, "This kind does not go out except by prayer and fasting" (Matthew 17:21 NKJV). What this boy had in his life was a stronghold of the devil, but a stronghold is just that: a strong *hold*. Praying while fasting is a gateway to see the power of God breaking down these walls, especially in times when we alone are powerless.

2. *Is it not to share your bread with the hungry and bring the homeless poor into your house; when you see the naked, to cover him, and not to hide yourself from your own flesh?*

   The Lord then shares that when we fast, it is so we can embrace His heart for the destitute. When we see those who are in lack, the hunger of our stomachs and the needs of our spirits enlighten us to their plight and give us the desire to share God's love for them, for the Lord is full of compassion and the desire to fill their lives with His goodness.

   God wants to work through us and make us a testimony of His love and grace. Thus, when we fast, forsaking pleasure and embracing His heart, we will begin to long for what He longs for and desire to take care of one another, to be a sign and a wonder of the good news to the destitute; God sincerely sees us, loves us, and cares for us.

3. *Then shall your light break forth like the dawn, and your healing shall spring up speedily; your righteousness shall go before you.*

   When we fast, we are breaking into the desire for our spiritual increase. First, our light will break forth like the dawn. Light is revelation. The eyes of our hearts will be enlightened in the knowledge of the Lord, and as we fast, we will see Him for who He is. Second, our healing will spring forth. Coming into salvation does not mean that we are instantly regenerated, renewed, healed, and delivered from all of our past; it is a process; as we fast, we are opening ourselves for physical, emotional, mental, and experiential healing. Last, our righteousness shall go before us. It says in Psalm 23:3, "He leads me in paths of righteousness for his name's sake" (ESV). Righteousness will be our forerunner. It will go before us to make every crooked path straight, and we will walk on the highway of righteousness.

4. *The glory of the Lord shall be your rear guard. Then you shall call, and the Lord will an-swer; you shall cry, and he will say, "Here I am."*

Finally, the greatest reward of them all is that by fasting and drawing ourselves nearer to God, He will increase His nearness to us. This verse tells us that the glory, majesty, beauty, splendor, and radiance of God will surround us and protect us. We will call out to Him, and He will answer, saying, "Here I am." It is not caused just by the sense of faith, but a sense of authentic and experiential nearness with Him. As we fast, setting our minds and hearts and focusing our prayers to His desires, Jesus says the Father will reward you (Matthew 6:17-18). I believe these are the greatest rewards that we could ever receive in this lifetime.

Fasting enlightens us to the weight of eternity. As we begin to develop spiritual hunger, we will begin to increase in the knowledge of eternal things rather than coveting earthly pleasures that are not worthy of our attraction. Therefore, we will walk in the awareness and power of "eternity in time" as we partner in accomplishing the will of God.

Fasting is sacrificing and putting oneself in a true place of weakness—fasting from social media is not one of these, being only a place of denial. We should take fasting seriously. When abstaining from food, we should be very cautious. However, caution does not mean compromise; it means consulting the Holy Spirit and being led by your Helper. The Lord is gracious, and when we consult the Holy Spirit, He will strengthen us for the physical woes of fasting and prayer.

There are many interpretations of prayer and fasting. I encourage you to weigh them all in light of the Word of God. I implore you to practice this out of obedience to the words of Christ, "When you fast," and in your pursuit of God.

Prayer and Worship

Second on the list is prayer and worship; prayer is our means of communing with God, and worship is the door. Scripture shows that the Lord takes worship very seriously. He states, "For you shall worship no other god, for the Lord, whose name is Jealous, is a jealous God" (Exodus 34:14). "Worship" simply means "what we adore." When we adore food, we express praise: "This is so good!" "Oh my goodness, this is to die for!" and so on. When we worship primetime television, we express praise: "That was such a good show!" "It was so funny!" "I think I'm going to watch that from now on."

The truth about worship is that nothing and no one deserves it more than God. Worship is our adoration, desire, and pursuit of God. We know what we worship by how much time we spend with it. Today, we worship iPhones, Facebook, Instagram, and Twitter. Spending time with God is not just consecrating a set time of day where you sing His praises. It is spending time with Him in your heart, in your conversations and activity. The Lord desires to accompany you in all affairs of life and to be your consistent guide, friend, and helper by His Spirit.

Worship magnifies the Lord. When God is exalted, everything else is lowered. Worship releases an awareness of the greatness of God. As Jesus says, "The hour is coming, and is now here, when the true worshipers will worship the Father in spirit and truth, for the Father is seeking such people to worship him. God is spirit, and those who worship him must worship in spirit and truth" (John 4:23-24). Worship attracts the inhabitance of God's presence and power (Psalm 22:3). It is the way before the Holy One (Psalm 100:4), and it is the key to an audience with God.

As we begin to pray, we should first worship the Lord and magnify Him. Our prayers go as deep as our worship. If we have carved a small image of God within ourselves, then we will only pray small prayers. But worship opens our spirits to the magnitude of God. It is like the ocean; when you are a far from it, you do not realize how vast and majestic it is. Worship is not just your vehicle to the ocean of the knowledge of God, but it is what plunges you into it. Worship reveals the vastness of His glorious splendor. When we begin to exalt Him, whether in word or song, we are introducing situations and the burdens of our hearts to the bigness of our God. Before we pray, we must continually introduce our hearts to the holiness of God. The word "holy" simply means, "above, sacred, and set apart." When entering into prayer, I like to think of the greatest physical wonder I can imagine, which is the universe above me, and in my heart, I see the glory of the Holy One reigning above it in all of His majesty!

The power of authentic worship is that it prepares for the revelation of God. Everything we read in the Word of God is filtered through our view of Him. Worship is not exclusively a song; it is the finite soul and spirit bowing in homage to the Eternal and Perfect God. Worship causes us to stand in awe of God. Thus, worship increases our faith and ability to believe.

I believe with all my heart that the Lord in now in the thick of resurrecting the tabernacle of David within you and me. The tabernacle of David was not filled with sacrifices of animals, but the sacrifices of expressive worship. The Lord promised in Amos 9:11, "In that day I will raise up the booth of David that is fallen and repair its breaches, and raise up its ruins and rebuild it as in the days of old." Then James, in Acts 15:14-18, filled with the Holy Spirit, writes:

> *Simeon has related how God first visited the Gentiles, to take from them a people for his name. And with this the words of the prophets agree, just as it is written, "After this I will return, and I will rebuild the tent of David that has fallen; I will rebuild its ruins, and I will restore it, that the remnant of mankind may seek the Lord, and all the Gentiles who are called by my name, says the Lord, who makes these things known from of old."*

We are called to this same remnant James is referring to. The Lord has taken us for His name!

We discussed in earlier chapters that we are priests before God, and since Christ has fulfilled the ceremonial offering, it is now our privilege to sacrifice spiritual offerings to God. Scripture states:

> *Through him then let us continually offer up a sacrifice of praise to God, that is, the fruit of lips that acknowledge his name. Do not neglect to do good and to share what you have, for such sacrifices are pleasing to God. (Hebrews 13:15-16)*

Also:

> *You yourselves like living stones are being built up as a spiritual house, to be a holy priesthood, to offer spiritual sacrifices acceptable to God through Jesus Christ. But you are a chosen race, a royal priesthood, a holy nation, a people for his own possession, that you may proclaim the excellencies of him who called you out of darkness into his marvelous light. Once you were not a people, but now you are God's people; once you had not received mercy, but now you have received mercy.* (1 Peter 2:5, 9-10)

And lastly:

> *I appeal to you therefore, brothers, by the mercies of God, to present your bodies as a living sacrifice, holy and acceptable to God, which is your spiritual worship. Do not be conformed to this world, but be transformed by the renewal of your mind, that by testing you may discern what is the will of God, what is good and acceptable and perfect.* (Romans 12:1-2)

Therefore, our communion, unity, increase of revelation, and inner renewal go as deep as our spiritual worship before God. Again, our prayers are as deep as our worship.

Please set this book down for a moment and worship God. Declare His majesty and holiness! Consult the psalms of David and the book of Revelations if you run out of words; just minister to Him. He is absolutely worthy of every good thing we can offer to Him. Yield to the Holy Spirit and praise Him in the tongue of mysteries (if you have one), and be led by the Holy Spirit even in words you cannot understand. Praise and worship the Lord!

Prayer and Prophecy

Against the popular movement of "prophecy refinement," I believe God is releasing John the Baptists who will speak and restore the words, "Thus saith the Lord." What we see in the body of Christ today is the prophecy refinement movement, which diminishes the weight of prophecy. We have lost confidence in the spoken Word of the Lord and thus neglect it. We now are more comfortable telling people, "We feel like this is what God is saying," rather than the true form of bold prophecy that we witness in Scripture. Isaiah 30:10-11 reveals to us what we are doing:

> *Who say to the seers, "Do not see," and to the prophets, "Do not prophesy to us what is right; speak to us smooth things, prophesy illusions, leave the way, turn aside from the path, let us hear no more about the Holy One of Israel."*

Jonah did not go to Nineveh and say, "This is what I feel like the Lord is saying." No, he declared, "Yet forty days, and Nineveh shall be overthrown" (Jonah 3:4). Subsequently, "The people of Nineveh believed God" (Jonah 3:5). The prophets, above all of their supernatural functions that we see in the OT and NT, are intercessors. The place of prayer was where they received the unction, words, boldness, and power to prophesy. Prayer and prophecy are both pillars to personal and corporate edification, exhortation, and encouragement. I believe the Lord is now making available and reestablishing the weight and power that prophecy should have as we dedicate ourselves to prayer.

Lastly, let us explore the dynamics of prophecy in prayer. Prophecy is given for direction. We know by OT and NT Scripture that prophecy brings clarity and direction and provides guidance and correction. Paul states in 1 Corinthians 14:1, 3-5:

> *Pursue love, and earnestly desire the spiritual gifts, especially that you may prophesy. The one who prophesies speaks to people for their upbuilding and encouragement and consolation. The one who speaks in a tongue builds up himself, but the one who prophesies builds up the church. Now I want you all to speak in tongues, but even more to prophesy. The one who prophesies is greater than the one who speaks in tongues, unless someone interprets, so that the church may be built up.*

Paul encourages us to earnestly seek the manifestations of the Holy Spirit, but especially to prophesy. Prophecy is shown to be three distinctive gifts of the Holy Spirit, that is, word of knowledge (supernaturally knowing something by the Holy Spirit), word of wisdom (knowing what to do and say by the Holy Spirit), and spiritual discernment (the ability to spiritually recognize the difference spirits). As shown in Scripture, these gifts are the fundamentals of the prophecy gift.

Like intercession, prophecy is a tool to direct sinners towards the kingdom. 1 Corinthians 14:24-25 states this truth: "If all prophesy, and an unbeliever or outsider enters, he is convicted by all, he is called to account by all, the secrets of his heart are disclosed, and so, falling on his face, he will worship God and declare that God is really among you." When we prophesy, we confront the sinner and bring him into the testimony of the realness of God and Christ.

Prophecy enlightens us to the revelation of Jesus, for as stated in Revelation 19:10, "For the testimony of Jesus is the spirit of prophecy." The power of this statement is that prophecy reveals who Jesus is. John experienced the time of his life as prophecy after prophecy was given and revelation after revelation of Jesus was exposed to him. God releasing prophecy in the earth prepares us and opens our eyes to receive the testimony of Christ.

Prophecy can only be given, received, and interpreted by the Holy Spirit. As Scripture states in 2 Peter 1:19-21:

> *And we have the prophetic word more fully confirmed, to which you will do well to pay attention as to a lamp shining in a dark place, until the day dawns and the morning star rises in your hearts, knowing this first of all, that no prophecy of Scripture comes from someone's own interpretation. For no prophecy was ever produced by the will of man, but men spoke from God as they were carried along by the Holy Spirit.*

Prayer is our means of fellowship with the Holy Spirit and when we hear words of prophecy being released we will be "carried along" by the Holy Spirit into its power, revelation, or to see its falsehood. Prayer enlightens our eyes to receive the spirit of wisdom and revelation. Therefore, the discernment for prophecy is received as we excel and grow in the knowledge of the Lord. We see many pastors and parishioners alike who, out of fear because of the presence of prophetic falsehood, stifle all prophecy even when it is authentic. I believe that the weakness of the Church that we see today is because of the stifling of the prophetic. The Word of the Lord is being stifled in the Church, which only results in our lack of growth in hearing and obeying the Word.

Prophecy encourages, and encouragement brings life to the heart. As Scripture states, "A man's spirit will endure sickness, but a crushed spirit who can bear?" (Proverbs 18:14). When the Lord prophesied to Israel, whenever it was of good report, they rejoiced and continued in the way of the Lord. When it was a bad report and they did not repent, we see in Scripture that the people were given over to their enemies, and they were found mourning with crushed spirits. Prophecy, when fulfilled, rejuvenates the soul and revives trust in the faithfulness of God. It says in Psalm 19:7-9:

> *The law of the Lord is perfect, reviving the soul; the testimony of the Lord is sure, making wise the simple; the precepts of the Lord are right, rejoicing the heart; the commandment of the Lord is pure, enlightening the eyes; the fear of the Lord is clean, enduring forever; the rules of the Lord are true, and righteous altogether.*

Prophecy is a part of releasing and reviving the law, testimony, precepts, and commandments of God: the fear of the Lord and the rules of His kingdom. When we pray and are carried along by the Holy Spirit, we begin to release the power of God as we speak prophetically. Prophecy builds us up, increases the knowledge of the Lord, and elevates our power and our hope, restoring trust and reviving our hearts to go for the things of God.

Prayer is a two-way street; we speak and we listen, and then we repeat. When we pray for the fulfillment of His word and will, we are prophesying to our lives and to the earth. As Scripture says:

> *And it shall come to pass afterward, that I will pour out my Spirit on all flesh; your sons and your daughters shall prophesy, your old men shall dream dreams, and your young men shall see visions. Even on the male and female servants in those days I will pour out my Spirit.* (Joel 2:28-29)

Then Peter in Acts 2:16-18 says:

> *But this is what was uttered through the prophet Joel: "And in the last days it shall be, God declares, that I will pour out my Spirit on all flesh, and your sons and your daughters shall prophesy, and your young men shall see visions, and your old men shall dream dreams; even on my male servants and female servants in those days I will pour out my Spirit, and they shall prophesy."*

And Paul in Romans 8:19 says, "For the creation waits with eager longing for the revealing of the sons of God." The sign of the sons of God, as Scripture encourages, is the manifestation of prophecy by the Holy Spirit.

Recap

The Lord wants to speak throughout the earth through the Church. Prayer releases the Spirit of God to fill us with the boldness to prophesy. The early Church prayed:

> *"And now, Lord, look upon their threats and grant to your servants to continue to speak your word with all boldness, while you stretch out your hand to heal, and signs and wonders are performed through the name of your holy servant Jesus." And when they had prayed, the place in which they were gathered together was shaken, and they were all filled with the Holy Spirit and continued to speak the Word of God with boldness.* (Acts 4:29-3)

I pray the insight in this book will thrust you deeper into all that prayer has for you. I pray this over you:

> *That the God of our Lord Jesus Christ, the Father of glory, may give you the Spirit of wisdom and of revelation in the knowledge of him, having the eyes of your hearts enlightened, that you may know what is the hope to which he has called you, what are the riches of his glorious inheritance in the saints, and what is the immeasurable greatness of his power toward us who believe, according to the working of his great might that he worked in Christ when he raised him from the dead and seated him at his right hand in the heavenly places, far above all rule and authority and power and dominion, and above every name that is named, not only in this age but also in the one to come. And he put all things under his feet and gave him as head over all things to the church, which is his body, the fullness of him who fills all in all.* (Ephesians 1:17-23)

CHAPTER 10

Releasing the Power of God

Healing

This chapter is more about receiving the anointing of the Holy Spirit and equipping oneself with the insights of the anointing received as we dedicate our lives to prayer. When we do this, we are dedicating our lives to be consumed by God's presence. We dedicate our lives to the hand of God resting on us, so that when we walk away from both our hidden and corporate fellowship with Him, we move in power to transform the world. In prayer, our minds become His counsel room, our hearts His throne, our bodies truly consecrated as the temple of His presence, and our atmospheres a canopy for His glory.

In the gospel of Luke, Jesus is shown to be a healer; Luke, being a physician, paid special attention to this power because he was intrigued by His supernatural ability to heal. Luke records in chapter 5:15-17, "Great crowds gathered to hear him and to be healed of their infirmities. But he would withdraw to desolate places and pray.... And the power of the Lord was with him to heal" (ESV).

Luke saw that Jesus' power to heal was connected to His prayer life, and even the disciples realized that the power of Jesus' ministry was a product. The disciples never asked Jesus to teach them how to preach, prophesy, or even heal the sick; the only time they requested teaching is when they asked Him, "Lord, teach us to pray, as John taught his disciples" (Luke 11:1). We are granted this power in the same way. In prayer and fellowshipping with the Lord, we receive the power to heal. The disciples dedicated themselves to this same model of dedication to prayer, and from that place, the ministry of the Word.

Jesus had an understanding of His relationship with the Lord and, flowing from that place of relationship, His authority to perform amazing works and teach with power, as He stated to the disciples in John 5:19-21:

> *Truly, truly, I say to you, the Son can do nothing of his own accord, but only what he sees the Father doing. For whatever the Father does, that the Son does likewise. For the Father loves the Son and shows him all that he himself is doing. And greater works than these will he show him, so that you may marvel. For as the Father raises the dead and gives them life, so also the Son gives life to whom he will.*

In the record of Lazarus' resurrection, Jesus models the idea of receiving from the Lord in prayer before acting. Lazarus was dead for four days before Jesus arrived, and Scripture says that Jesus prayed before the Father in front of the tomb. With the power that was invested into Him, He then raised Lazarus from the dead (John 11:1-44).

Power is linked to prayer, as I have experienced personally. When I dedicate myself to prayer, there seems to be a special grace upon me to heal. One time, I was in conversation with a young woman by the name of Misty. She explained to me that the doctors saw a tumor in her breast nine months prior to our conversation and that they were going to check again in a couple days. There arose in me a boldness and faith that was immoveable, and I prayed a five second prayer for her healing and told her to not fear or say anything else to anyone, to just believe in the power of God to heal her. The following week, I saw her, and she hugged me, crying. I thought to myself, "The tumor is still there." But then she showed me a photo of two sets of X-rays. The earlier set showed the tumor, and the other showed nine X-rays with no tumor whatsoever. The doctors were amazed and called it "spontaneous degeneration," but I know the healing power of the Lord was involved.

I hear about many believers trying to shortcut their way to healing power, but there is no shortcut. Jesus could heal because He honored the process of power. As we devote ourselves to prayer, we too link ourselves to the healing power of God, just as the signs and wonders that the apostles performed were linked to devoting themselves to the place of prayer:

> And they devoted themselves to the apostles' teaching and the fellowship, to the breaking of bread and the prayers. And awe came upon every soul, and many wonders and signs were being done through the apostles. (Acts 2:42-43)

In the place of prayer, ask the Lord to allow the power to heal to be with you. Ask Him to release demonstrations of the Spirit and of power as you minster the word. Do not leave witnessing to the "evangelist"—we are all called to the ministry of the Word, and God endorses His message by releasing His power through us to reveal His glory. Infiltrate Walmart, Target, and Best Buy with the testimony of Christ, and be followed by signs, wonders, and miracles. I pray that the anointing of God to heal the sick will be released. In Jesus' Name.

Deliverance

When we dedicate ourselves to the place of prayer, we receive the power to deliver. Jesus, being accused by the religious official of casting out devils by the devil, states in Scripture:

> Every kingdom divided against itself is laid waste, and no city or house divided against itself will stand. And if Satan casts out Satan, he is divided against himself. How then will his kingdom stand? And if I cast out demons by Beelzebul, by whom do your sons cast them out? Therefore they will be your judges. But if it is by the Spirit of God that I cast out demons, then the kingdom of God has come upon you. (Matthew 12:25-28)

I have already mentioned that Jesus found the power to do miracles by receiving from the Father from a place of prayer. Jesus logically explains that He cannot cast out demons by Satan because that means Satan is working against his own plan to subdue and oppress God's creation. Jesus says that He was casting out devils by the power of the Spirit of God for the sake of the kingdom. Many times, He cast out demons for the sake of healing someone; for example, "a demon-oppressed man who was blind and mute was brought to him, and he healed him, so that the man spoke and saw" (Matthew 12:22). The Lord cast out a demon to heal the infirmity. Thus, when we receive the power to heal, we also receive the same power to deliver.

The power to deliver exists for the sake of advancing the kingdom of God and bringing desolation to the kingdom of darkness. When we dedicate ourselves to the place of prayer, the Lord's power to heal is the same power we operate in to cast out devils and bring deliverance to victims of the kingdom of darkness. Scripture also shows us two dangers that the place of prayer protects us from: not knowing Christ, and demons not knowing us. First, Jesus states:

> *Not everyone who says to me, "Lord, Lord," will enter the kingdom of heaven, but the one who does the will of my Father who is in heaven. On that day many will say to me, "Lord, Lord, did we not prophesy in your name, and cast out demons in your name, and do many mighty works in your name?" And then will I declare to them, "I never knew you; depart from me, you workers of lawlessness." (Matthew 7:21-23)*

This passage says that many will say they have done many works in Jesus' name; however, the problem is that they did not know Jesus. It is possible to know and witness the power of the name of Jesus, but we receive the ultimate reward of eternity not by deeds but by a relationship with God through His Spirit, which the place of prayer secures. The name of Jesus works all by itself, but there is a danger for those who do not know Him, as shown in Acts 19:13-17:

> *Some of the itinerant Jewish exorcists undertook to invoke the name of the Lord Jesus over those who had evil spirits, saying, "I adjure you by the Jesus whom Paul proclaims." Seven sons of a Jewish high priest named Sceva were doing this. But the evil spirit answered them, "Jesus I know, and Paul I recognize, but who are you?" And the man in whom was the evil spirit leaped on them, mastered all of them and overpowered them, so that they fled out of that house naked and wounded.*

By the name of Christ, the demons came out, but because the sons of Sceva did not know the Lord and tried to shortcut the process of power, they ended up being the ones who needed deliverance. They witnessed the power of the name of Jesus, but it is a relationship with the Lord that protects.

The place of prayer brings us into the power of God. It was said of Jesus in Luke 2:52, "And Jesus increased in wisdom and in stature and in favor with God and man." If Jesus in His earthly ministry had to increase and grow in these, we must do the same. Salvation does not promise us power; it is the entrance to the new covenant, which promises eternity with the Lord.

The disciples, who physically walked with Jesus, did not release the power for them to witness His glory, but Jesus said in Acts 1:8, "You will receive power when the Holy Spirit has come upon you, and you will be my witnesses in Jerusalem and in all Judea and Samaria, and to the end of the earth." Salvation does come through believing in the testimony of the Lord, and the disciples witnessed Him and His resurrection, so they did believe; but Jesus still told them to wait for the Holy Spirit, for only then would they have the power to be His witnesses. They obeyed, waiting for the promise of the Holy Spirit in that place of prayer, "And suddenly there came from heaven a sound like a mighty rushing wind, and it filled the entire house where they were sitting. And divided tongues as of fire appeared to them and rested on each one of them. And they were all filled with the Holy Spirit and began to speak in other tongues as the Spirit gave them utterance" (Acts 2:2-4). Because they obeyed, waited, and prayed, they received the power promised to them.

Power in prayer will many times come through the "suddenlies" of the Spirit. Many times, I have prayed and did not "feel" the power of God, but as I kept seeking the Lord, the Spirit would seem to suddenly break in and fill me afresh. It will seem as if we can be in prayer for a long time before the power of the Spirit comes upon us; Jesus waited 30 years before the affirmation of the Father and the Spirit came upon Him, and then He was in the wilderness for 40 days, returning often to desolate places to be refilled. We do not know how long the disciples were in the place of prayer, but we know that in their obedience to Jesus, power suddenly came upon them. A blinded Saul of Tarsus fasted and prayed for three days after His vision of the resurrected Lord before He regained his sight and received the gift of the Holy Spirit. From their examples, we must learn to pray until we receive power.

I pray the hand of God be upon you to deliver people in the possession of darkness and bring plunder to the enemy's treasury. I pray that you and the finger of God become one. In Jesus' Name.

Discernment

When it comes to releasing the power of God, we must operate in spiritual discernment. What we must not do is enter into spiritual things with an un-renewed mindset. As we become closer to the Lord, we will begin to operate more and more in the counsel of the Spirit, resulting in the sharpening of our discernment. When Jesus says in John 5:19 that "the Son can do nothing of his own accord, but only what he sees the Father doing. For whatever the Father does, that the Son does likewise," He is stating an amazing truth; Jesus, even though He was speaking of Himself, is revealing to us the nature of our relationship: "I do what I see my Father do." Jesus in His earthly ministry was one with the Father, the Father was in Him by the Holy Spirit and the He was in the Father through the same Spirit; after Jesus was urged by the religious officials to give them a sign because of their unbelief, He answers:

> *I and the Father are one. If I am not doing the works of my Father, then do not believe me; but if I do them, even though you do not believe me, believe the works that you may know and understand that the Father is in me and I am in the Father.* (John 10:30, 37-38)

Similarly, as we are led by the Holy Spirit, we are sons and daughters—joint-heirs with Christ; for that reason, we walk in the inheritance of God. For again, as Romans 8:14-17 states:

> *For all who are led by the Spirit of God are sons of God. For you did not receive the spirit of slavery to fall back into fear, but you have received the Spirit of adoption as sons, by whom we cry, "Abba! Father!" The Spirit himself bears witness with our spirit that we are children of God, and if children, then heirs—heirs of God and fellow heirs with Christ, provided we suffer with him in order that we may also be glorified with him.*

Therefore, we know by faith that we have also inherited the power to do the works Jesus did on earth. Jesus himself even declares, "Truly, truly, I say to you, whoever believes in me will also do the works that I do; and greater works than these will he do, because I am going to the Father" (John 14:12). Having inherited such power, we must operate with the same spiritual logic and discernment that Christ operated in.

Discernment is also needed to counsel us on whether we need to speak healing or demand deliverance. This discernment is inherited inside the place of prayer and closeness to the Lord and will let us know from what to ask for deliverance. Spiritual discernment gives us a sense of boldness and faith; by the Spirit, we have the ability to distinguish between spirits of sickness—to which we speak healing—and the spirits of oppression—to which we demand deliverance—there will be an assurance and boldness that rises within our hearts, making us immovable by doubt, releasing unwavering faith.

Scripture tells us Jesus was moved by compassion, and He worked miracles for the advancement of God's kingdom. We also must not apprehend the working of miracles, but comprehend that it is for the sake of the advancement of the kingdom. Jesus wants us to exercise the authority He has given us in the kingdom, for we have inherited power from God to heal the sick, raise the dead, and cast out demons.

Recap

In the place of prayer, our inheritance is the power to heal the sick and hurting and to deliver the oppressed. We must operate in spiritual discernment, which means following the lead of the Holy Spirit. Jesus' simplicity is what we need to function by; if someone is sick, heal them, for by the Spirit of God, we have inherited the power to do so, and we know that signs, wonders, and miracles are the greater works that Christ has commissioned us to do. As Jesus said, "For as the Father raises the dead and gives them life, also the Son gives life to whom He wills."

It was the decision of Christ to heal the sick, deliver the oppressed, and raise the dead; therefore, we understand by faith that it is for the advancement of the kingdom. When someone is delivered from the enemy's possession, whether it be from disease, depression, or even perversion and condemnation, we know they are to be brought out of darkness so that the kingdom of light may expand and the testimony of God's power and love in the earth can flood the nations.

May the Lord be with you and reveal Himself to you. May the Lord, as you seek Him diligently, give you your inheritance. I pray that the Father will give you divine wisdom, insight, directive counsel, supernatural understanding, and discernment. I pray that He will increase your capacity for greater sensitivity to the Holy Spirit and the holistic operation of your Spirit-given gifts and talents. I pray that the Lord will thrust your mind into the mind-sphere of the supernatural and give you power and the ability to see the manifestation of His glory in all your ways. In Jesus' Name.

CHAPTER 11

Spiritual Warfare

Declare War

Beloved, I hope you are being matured in the understanding of the place of prayer, for it is in our dedication to pray that the anointing of God is released. This chapter's goal is, firstly, to inform you how, by intercession through prayer, we are engaging in spiritual warfare against the kingdom of Satan; secondly, to share a brief yet impactful exposition on our weapons of warfare; and lastly, to expose how deceitful the enemy is.

When stepping into the place of prayer, specifically intercession, we are provoking the enemy to war. Inasmuch as our intercession is bringing forth holy change in the world and we are bringing desolation to the kingdom of darkness, do not be fooled into thinking that the enemy is not going to retaliate. Our battle is not against governmental politics or against any human being; according to Scripture, our warfare is against spiritual forces of evil: principalities, authorities, powers over present darkness, and evil spirits in the heavenly places (Ephesians 6:12).

I caution you to not think of this as strange or as "fiction mysticism." Just as oxygen is ever-moving and active, though we do not see it, so is the spiritual world; and a part of the enemy's plan is to infiltrate cultures to train minds to believe he and the spiritual world are not real. Thus, we see in entertainment, shows, and movies messages that deceive hearts, lessening awareness of his plans, powers, and influence. Scripture calls Satan "the prince of the power of the air" (Ephesians 2:2 NKJV) and "the god of this age" (2 Corinthians 4:4), and there is an anti-Christ spirit saying that even Christ is fictional. This same agenda floods even the Church. All kinds of doctrines of devils are invading the pulpit, teaching against the things of God rather than for them. Still, the Lord still has a remnant that has not abandoned the true Word of God—the gospel of Christ, which remains our salvation through Jesus.

Through prayer, we have the power to infiltrate and displace demonic powers, agendas, systems, and influences in the earth, and by our intercession, we confront demonic principalities. The word "principality" means "a state ruled by a prince," and in the hierarchy of the demonic kingdom, principalities come first. As said before, Satan is called "the prince of the power of the air," which denotes one of these territories, and according to passages like Daniel 10:13, 20, demonic princes can rule over whole regions or nations. Principalities are set to maintain or govern a specific agenda; for example, the principality over Islamic nations is the anti-Christ agenda. These territories serve as obstacles in the spiritual realm; for instance, in Daniel 10, when Daniel was receiving revelation of the end times and Gabriel was sent to give him understanding, the prince of the kingdom of Persia was sent to hinder that understanding. But just as there are demonic princes, there are also angelic ones; in that same chapter, Michael is called one of the Chief Princes, and he is mentioned by Gabriel to have assisted in the fight against the prince of the kingdom of Persia. This is what happens in the spiritual realm when we pray. Thus, when we begin to intercede for the ministry of the gospel, asking the Father to open doors into other nations, we are confronting the principalities that govern those nations.

Under those principalities, there are set powers or authorities of the present darkness, and by intercession, we gain the authority to displace this power. Powers or authorities are spirits who exercise their power in the human affairs of the world (Ephesians 2:2; 3:10). These evil spirits' purpose is to set the course of wickedness in the humans who are of power or authority in a nation, like in the days of Ahab, when an evil spirit was given "authority" over the Ahab's prophets to cause them to prophesy lies (1 Kings 22:19-23). Our prayers are like the intercession of Elijah the prophet against the prophets of Baal; he displaced the demonic power under whose authority they prophesied and displayed the glory of God's power. By our intercession, we serve an eviction notice to the demonic powers and authorities. This also directly relates to the previous chapter on Christ's advocacy in the heavenly council:

When we pray, asking God for access, our prayers invoke the assembly of the divine council. Christ as King of His cause stands to advocate in the heavenly court on our behalf as we also intercede, though Satan rages against it. The Church, the embassy of Christ's kingdom, is struggling to bring the gospel to the Middle East and other hostile areas due to demonic "powers" harshly hindering us, but we perceive by our partnership with the legalities decreed in heaven that the council rules in favor of our authority to possess these territories for the Gospel due to Christ inheriting legal rights to be lifted up there. Thus, we pursue these areas for the glory of Christ, while declaring to those same demonic authorities and rulers of the age that their powers over the nation are evicted.

Also, by our intercession, we entreat spiritual reaction. As humans, we do not have the power in and of ourselves to fight against unholy angels, but we do have all authority by Christ, who states in Matthew 16:18-19, "On this rock I will build my church, and the gates of hell shall not prevail against it. I will give you the keys of the kingdom of heaven, and whatever you bind on earth shall be bound in heaven, and whatever you loose on earth shall be loosed in heaven" (ESV). Hebrews 1:14 adds, "Are they not all ministering spirits, sent forth to do service for the sake of them that shall inherit salvation?" Through our intercession, Christ and His angels engage against Satan and his angels; the armies of the kingdom of heaven are set to war against the evil powers on our behalf. The Bible gives an example through the story of Joshua:

When Joshua was by Jericho, he lifted up his eyes and looked, and behold, a man was standing before him with his drawn sword in his hand. And Joshua went to him and said to him, "Are you for us, or for our adversaries?" And he said, "No; but I am the commander of the army of the Lord. Now I have come." (Joshua 5:13-14)

This passage shows that when we pray according to the Lord's plan, we are invoking angelic help to engage in warfare on our behalf. We have the power to cast out devils when they infiltrate our dimension, but in the heavenly places, the Lord has all authority, and as we pray according to His will, we authorize the power of His angels to minister for our sake. By our intercession, we demolish the stronghold of the enemy.

Make War

Despite our allies, the enemy will retaliate and try to deceive, distract, and weaken us. Before we get into some insights of how the enemy tries to do this, let us discuss the weapons of our warfare against him. Paul in Ephesians 6:13-18 states,

Therefore take up the whole armor of God, that you may be able to withstand in the evil day, and having done all, to stand firm. Stand therefore, having fastened on the belt of truth, and having put on the breastplate of righteousness, and, as shoes for your feet, having put on the readiness given by the gospel of peace. In all circumstances take up the shield of faith, with which you can extinguish all the flaming darts of the evil one; and take the helmet of salvation, and the sword of the Spirit, which is the word of God, praying at all times in the Spirit, with all prayer and supplication. To that end keep alert with all perseverance, making supplication for all the saints.

Paul says we have armor that the Lord provides, which makes us able to withstand the evilness of our day. We must live in the integrity of truth and the fortification of the truth of Christ. We must live in the righteousness of God that cannot be achieved but by the applied grace of the Lord bought by the blood of Christ and through fellowship with the Holy Spirit. We must be prepared with the gospel of God's surpassing peace. Armed with salvation that is obtained by receiving and only receiving Christ as our Lord; faith that is developed by reading, hearing, studying and speaking the Word of God; and praying always by the direction and expression given through our bond with the Holy Spirit. But I would like to speak of two other weapons we have that are developed within our lives by the help of the Holy Spirit:

1. Consistency

The greatest tactic of the enemy is compromise. Paul encourages us to "withstand...and having done all, to stand firm" (Ephesians 6:13). Here, Scripture is telling us to be consistent. What we are inwardly facing in the Church today is the lack of consistency: consistency in prayer, in assembling with one another, in faith, and ultimately in Christ. Today, we lack patience in everything, so if one thing takes too long, we move on to something else. For this reason, a lot of believers around the world have not endured the process of rooting themselves in the knowledge of Christ; they lack maturity, causing division, dissension, and stagnancy. Abraham was promised a child 25 years before received Isaac; Abraham was consistent in faith even when it did not seem like the promise was to come to pass. We should learn to follow his example of steadfastness and patience.

To be a disciple means to be a disciplined and consistent follower and learner; therefore, we must fortify ourselves by being consistent at all costs. James 1:2-4 tells us that by consistency we will be made perfect and complete, lacking nothing: "Count it all joy, my brothers, when you meet trials of various kinds, for you know that the testing of your faith produces steadfastness. And let steadfastness have its full effect, that you may be perfect and complete, lacking in nothing." Scripture also states that patience is one of the fruits of the Spirit (Galatians 5:22).

There is no room for compromise in a disciplined and consistent heart. We will see many victories in spiritual warfare if we remain consistent in faith, in prayer and intercession, in hope, in fellowship with the Holy Spirit, and in the Word of the Lord.

2. Love

Secondly, love is a wonderful remedy for the division that the enemy tries to cause amongst us, which is shown in the famous "love chapter" in the New Testament:

> *If I speak in the tongues of men and of angels, but have not love, I am a noisy gong or a clanging cymbal. And if I have prophetic powers, and understand all mysteries and all knowledge, and if I have all faith, so as to remove mountains, but have not love, I am nothing. If I give away all I have, and if I deliver up my body to be burned, but have not love, I gain nothing. Love is patient and kind; love does not envy or boast; it is not arrogant or rude. It does not insist on its own way; it is not irritable or resentful; it does not rejoice at wrongdoing, but rejoices with the truth. Love bears all things, believes all things, hopes all things, endures all things. Love never ends. As for prophecies, they will pass away; as for tongues, they will cease; as for knowledge, it will pass away.* (1 Corinthians 13:1-8)

Spiritual gifts and abilities do not trump love. Love is our most powerful weapon as we wage war against the enemy, because it is by love that we abide in the Lord. As 1 John 4:7-8 states:

> *Beloved, let us love one another, for love is from God, and whoever loves has been born of God and knows God. Anyone who does not love does not know God, because God is love.*

Love never fails, and whoever abides in God love will abide in love. The power of love is found in our choices. We choose to love even when the feelings of affection ebb. In love, we find patience, kindness, selflessness, a lack of enviousness or the need to be arrogant or rude, a lack of resentment, the ability to choose not to be irritable, the disposition not to rejoice in wrongdoing, the strength to bear all things, and the ability to hope in all situations. When we live in love, anything from Satan—things like pride, doubt and condemnation—is absolutely repulsive to us.

The greatest understanding I have ever received and the greatest treasure to me is that though the Lord loves and has befriended me through His Spirit, He is still the Sovereign Lord, God of all creation, and is worthy to be feared. Many doctrines of this age, invading even the Church, are teaching more against the fear of the Lord by lessening the weight of the nature of its revelation. Think about what the Word says about Him; He is a consuming fire; at the sight of Him, the prophets who witnessed His awesomeness trembled in fear or fainted. In Exodus 20:18, 20 it states:

> *Now when all the people saw the thunder and the flashes of lightning and the sound of the trumpet and the mountain smoking, the people were afraid and trembled, and they stood far off. Moses said to the people, "Do not fear, for God has come to test you, that the fear of him may be before you, that you may not sin."*

It is the fear of the Lord that keeps us from transgressing against Him. We will stand before God, and He will not judge us by our good intentions. How we live our lives and what we choose to do is either rooted in the fear of the Lord—to hate what He hates and love what He loves—or is not; if it is the latter, we end up not bearing anything of worth in our lives. All of our works done outside of this knowledge and reverential fear of God will be as wood, hay, and straw in His fire of judgment. For as shown in 1 Corinthians 3:10-15, it is when we live in a healthy reverence and honor of God that we ascribe glory to Him, and our works will be proven to be like precious metals that will not burn:

> *According to the grace of God given to me, like a skilled master builder I laid a foundation, and someone else is building upon it. Let each one take care how he builds upon it. For no one can lay a foundation other than that which is laid, which is Jesus Christ. Now if anyone builds on the foundation with gold, silver, precious stones, wood, hay, straw—each one's work will become manifest, for the Day will disclose it, because it will be revealed by fire, and the fire will test what sort of work each one has done. If the work that anyone has built on the foundation survives, he will receive a reward. If anyone's work is burned up, he will suffer loss, though he himself will be saved, but only as through fire.*

The fear of the Lord is imperative to us as believers. Without the fear of the Lord, we will live and work carelessly. I encourage you to ask the Lord to open your heart to see His awesomeness, and the things of this world will grow strange to you in comparison to His glory. When we fear the Lord, living a righteous and holy life will soon follow. Proverbs 29:27 states about the righteous, "An unjust man is an abomination to the righteous, but one whose way is straight is an abomination to the wicked." When the fear of the Lord is in our hearts, the unrighteous way is an abomination, meaning it is repulsive to sight and thought.

As said of Jesus in Isaiah 11:2-3, "And the Spirit of the Lord shall rest upon him, the Spirit of wisdom and understanding, the Spirit of counsel and might, the Spirit of knowledge and the fear of the Lord. And his delight shall be in the fear of the Lord." This same Spirit is within us; let us follow the heart of Jesus and delight in the fear of the Lord, for it will keep us from the crooked paths of darkness.

The Devil is A Liar

The devil is a liar. It sounds old school, but simple truths stand the test of time! Satan, being the father of lies, is the god of this world, and he has the world deceived. Jesus states of those who do not follow God, "You are of your father the devil, and your will is to do your father's desires. He was a murderer from the beginning, and does not stand in the truth, because there is no truth in him. When he lies, he speaks out of his own character, for he is a liar and the father of lies" (John 8:44). In accordance with this, 2 Corinthians 4:4 states, "In their case the god of this world has blinded the minds of the unbelievers, to keep them from seeing the light of the gospel of the glory of Christ, who is the image of God." The devil has one agenda, and that is to blind the world from the light of the gospel of Christ.

We live in a dying world, oppressed and depraved because of the spirit of this age. Even in the Church, the doctrines of devils seep into the hearts of our ministers, and those who are clearly living unholy lives are still allowed to minister because of their gifts and talents. We see un-rooted believers forsaking sound doctrine to satisfy themselves with illusions of truth. The enemy has sat in our pews and preached from our pulpits. He has compromised purity in the hearts of our ministers and seduced our ears to hear his smooth speech. The devil is a liar.

Beloved, the hour has come to war against the spirit of this age that is gaining territory in the Church. We must remember and know the truth of the Word of God. We must correct the lurking lies of the devil that have invaded sound biblical truths of holiness, faith, evangelism, prayer, and so on. We must not fear to stand for God and His Word, not just in the world, but also in the modern strains of a corrupted Christianity. We must rise with an awareness of Satan's devices and schemes and return to the Lord in prayer, receiving from Him the power to cast the devil and his lies out of the Church.

The enemy is getting us to compromise our responsibilities as the embassy of the kingdom of Christ, letting us be content with idleness, chasing prosperity for the sake of our own pleasure, and wasting our lifetime of purpose with good Sunday-morning Christianity. Do you not discern the presence of a snake is in our midst? We have become more concerned about living in the blessings of God for our own desires than truly being consumed with Jesus' heart for the world. We are more occupied with primetime television and our spiritual idolatry than we are with the work of the Kingdom.

The Lord confronted me and said, "If you love me, you will keep my commandments" (John 14:15). It is a selfish and deceptive idea to deny the call of God and believe that this life is about just having a "love affair" with Jesus. When this life becomes about our own satisfaction, we have sold our purpose to idleness, thus giving the devil more time to fulfill his desires in the earth.

The Lord is raising the call to return to the place of prayer, and the words of Joel the prophet ring in my heart:

"Yet even now," declares the Lord, "return to me with all your heart, with fasting, with weeping, and with mourning; and rend your hearts and not your garments." Return to the Lord your God, for he is gracious and merciful, slow to anger, and abounding in steadfast love; and he relents over disaster. Who knows whether he will not turn and relent, and leave a blessing behind him, a grain offering and a drink offering for the Lord your God?
(Joel 2:12-14)

It is only in returning with all our hearts to the Lord in the place of intercession that the lies from the devil will be exposed. Everything the world is partaking of according to his agenda will blind them to the gospel of Christ. Let not this same agenda continue to invade the Church. We must cast the devil from amongst us, get out of our paraplegic beds of compromise, complacency, and carnality, and return fully to the Lord, that we may know the power of His calling and truly fulfill our purpose on the earth.

We know by faith that we are in the thick of the birth pains of Christ's second coming. These are times of peril. Yet, I charge you to not to be like the foolish virgins who fell asleep as the bridegroom was passing by (Matthew 25:1-12). Will the Lord come in the earth and find faith? Will He come and find a ready bride? Will we continue to ignore the Lord and press the snooze button on intercession? Will we continue to hear His call to pray yet ignore it? Or will He come hearing the Spirit and the Bride saying, "Come"? Will we continue to see the need to fast and mourn for the condition of nations yet, continue to fill our stomachs to the full and never deny ourselves of slumber? Will the enemy continue to arouse us with his seductive reasoning, or will we arise in the knowledge of the fear of the Lord and bring to an end his lies?

Beloved, the coming of Christ is near, and we must not allow the anti-Christ spirit to possess the land, but instead, in the words of my namesake, "Let us go up at once and occupy it, for we are well able to overcome it" (Numbers 13:30). For John the apostle said this:

By this you know the Spirit of God: every spirit that confesses that Jesus Christ has come in the flesh is from God, and every spirit that does not confess Jesus is not from God. This is the spirit of the antichrist, which you heard was coming and now is in the world already. Little children, you are from God and have overcome them, for he who is in you is greater than he who is in the world. (1 John 4:2-4)

Recap

When we begin to engage in the business of prayer, we are declaring war against the wiles of darkness. Intercession is a spiritual tool of kingdom warfare. By intercession, we enter into a spiritual war; our weapons are not of the flesh, but of the spirit, backed by the power of God. When we intercede, we confront demonic principalities to subdue their powers on the earth. By this, we gain access to making disciples of all nations. The enemy retaliates with lies, deceit and foolishness, but we are protected by the Lord and His armor. We wage war by being consistent in our walk with the Lord, abounding in love to abide in God and delight in the fear of the Lord so that we do not sin and give a foothold to the enemy.

Beloved, pray without ceasing. I pray that the Lord will awaken you and release in you deep intercession. Allow the Holy Spirit to lead and guide you and give you utterance in prayer, for the time of His coming is near; we must assume our forerunner ministry and prepare the way of the Lord.

Farewell Blessings

My Prayer

Beloved, I love you, and my prayer is that you have come to understand the power of communion with God as you journeyed with me through this book. I hope you have been edified and encouraged to live your life as a child and true servant of God. Before I close, please pray these prayers with me:

The Knowledge of the Holy One

Father, as I delight in the fear of the Lord, by His Spirit, I pray that my eyes will be opened and my ears made attentive to the knowledge of the Holy One. I pray that the Lord be gracious and reveal Himself to me that I may be filled with the fullness of God. I pray You mold me into a person whom You can trust with the secrets and burdens of Your heart. Abba, I pray that You manifest and abide with me, fellowship with me, and increase your nearness right now. Accompany and lead me, Holy Spirit; take me by the hand and lead me into all truth. In Jesus' Name, thank You.

Power to Obey

Jesus, you said, "If you love me, keep my commandments." I thank you that I love you because you first loved me, and the Holy Spirit sheds the love of God in my heart. I pray that the same power to obey and keep the commandments of the Lord will also be upon me. I pray you baptize me afresh in the Holy Spirit and give me the power to be your witness in all my ways. I pray that the anointing of the Holy Spirit will be upon me, and that as I choose to venture deeper into this place of prayer, you will release utterance, Holy Spirit, and empower me.

Beloved, know that I am still praying for you. These following prayers, taken directly from Scripture, are for your benefit, that you might continue to walk in the calling of the Holy Spirit to advance the kingdom of God.

Apostolic Prayers

[I pray that] the God of our Lord Jesus Christ, the Father of glory, may give you the Spirit of wisdom and of revelation in the knowledge of him, having the eyes of your hearts enlightened, that you may know what is the hope to which he has called you, what are the riches of his glorious inheritance in the saints, and what is the immeasurable greatness of his power toward us who believe, according to the working of his great might that he worked in Christ when he raised him from the dead and seated him at his right hand in the heavenly places, far above all rule and authority and power and dominion, and above every name that is named, not only in this age but also in the one to come. And he put all things under his feet and gave him as head over all things to the church, which is his body, the fullness of him who fills all in all. (Ephesians 1:17-23)

It is my prayer that your love may abound more and more, with knowledge and all discernment, so that you may approve what is excellent, and so be pure and blameless for the day of Christ, filled with the fruit of righteousness that comes through Jesus Christ, to the glory and praise of God. (Philippians 1:9-11)

That you may be filled with the knowledge of his will in all spiritual wisdom and understanding, so as to walk in a manner worthy of the Lord, fully pleasing to him, bearing fruit in every good work and increasing in the knowledge of God; [may you be] strengthened with all power, according to his glorious might, for all endurance and patience with joy; giving thanks to the Father, who has qualified you to share in the inheritance of the saints in light. He has delivered us from the domain of darkness and transferred us to the kingdom of his beloved Son, in whom we have redemption, the forgiveness of sins. (Colossians 1:9-14)

May the God of endurance and encouragement grant you to live in such harmony with one another, in accord with Christ Jesus, that together you may with one voice glorify the God and Father of our Lord Jesus Christ. Therefore welcome one another as Christ has welcomed you, for the glory of God. May the God of hope fill you with all joy and peace in believing, so that by the power of the Holy Spirit you may abound in hope. (Romans 15:5-7, 13)

That our God may make you worthy of his calling and may fulfill every resolve for good and every work of faith by his power, so that the name of our Lord Jesus may be glorified in you, and you in him, according to the grace of our God and the Lord Jesus Christ. (2 Thessalonians 1:11-12)

In Jesus' mighty Name, so it must be for His exceeding glory.

Final Words

Beloved, pray also that the Word of the Lord in this book may run swiftly, that doors will be opened for these insights to be used for the encouragement, edification, exhortation, equipping, building up, and teaching of the body of Christ. May the love of God, the grace of the Lord Jesus Christ, and the fellowship of the Holy Spirit be with you all.

Works Cited

Books

Bevere, John. *The Holy Spirit: An Introduction.* Palmer Lake, CO: Messenger International, 2013. Print.

"G373 – "anapauō" - Strong's Greek Lexicon (KJV)." Blue Letter Bible. Web. 30 Sep, 2016.

"G3875 – "paraklētos" - Strong's Greek Lexicon (ESV)." Blue Letter Bible. Web. 30 Sep, 2016.

"H1605 – "ga`ar" - Strong's Hebrew Lexicon (KJV)." Blue Letter Bible. Web. 30 Sep, 2016.

Madden, Peter J. *The Wigglesworth Standard.* New Kensington, PA: Whitaker House, 2000. Print.

Oxford Dictionaries. "Advocacy." Def. 2. *Oxford Dictionaries.* Oxford University Press, Aug. 2015. Web. 20 Sept. 2015.

---. "Assignment." Def. 5. *Oxford Dictionaries.* Oxford University Press, Aug. 2015. Web. 20 Sept. 2015.

---. "Council." Def. 3. *Oxford Dictionaries.* Oxford University Press, Aug. 2015. Web. 20 Sept. 2015.

---. "Fasting." Def. 6. *Oxford Dictionaries.* Oxford University Press, Aug. 2015. Web. 20 Sept. 2016.

---. "Preeminence." Def. 1. *Oxford Dictionaries.* Oxford University Press, 2015. Web. 20 Sept. 2016

---. "Rebuke." Def. 4. *Oxford Dictionaries.* Oxford University Press, 2015. Web. 20 Sept. 2016

---. "Wisdom." Def. 7. *Oxford Dictionaries.* Oxford University Press, 2015. Web. 20 Sept. 2016

Russell, Corey. *Prayer: Why Our Words to God Matter.* Cork: BookBaby, 2013. Digital.

Wiersbe, Warren W. *Ephesians Through Revelation.* Vol. 2. Colorado Springs: David C. Cook, 2003. Print.

Additional Bible Translations Used

Scriptures by Chapter

Chapter 1: Personal Devotion

Quoted

Romans 8:26 (NKJV)	Jeremiah 17:10 (ESV)	Ephesians 3:17 (AMP)
Psalms 25:1-2 (NKJV)	1 John 4:16 (AMPC)	Colossians 1:26-27 (ESV)
Psalms 143:8 (NKJV)	Ephesians 3:14-19 (NKJV)	Jude 1:20 (NKJV)
Isaiah 29:13-14 (NLT)	Ephesians 3:14 (AMP)	Revelation 4:1 (NKJV)
1 John 4:8 (ESV)	Psalm 24:1 (ESV)	1 Corinthians 2:10-12 (NLT)
1 Samuel 16:7 (ESV)	Daniel 5:21 (NKJV)	Revelation 1:10 (NKJV)
Proverbs 21:2 (ESV)	1 Samuel 12:22 (NKJV)	Isaiah 60:1-5 (LEB)

Paraphrased, Restated, or Summarized

1 Corinthians 2:10-14	Hebrews 11:1	Genesis 3:8

Mentioned

2 Timothy 3:16-17	1 Corinthians 1:24	Revelation 21:6
John 14:26	2 Corinthians 5:15	John 4:24
John 1:1-14	Colossians 3:11	Genesis 1:26-27
John 14:6	1 John 2:2	

Chapter 2: Our Priestly Privilege

Quoted

Leviticus 17:11 (ESV)	Hebrews 10:19-23 (ESV)	1 Peter 1:13-16 (ESV)
Matthew 7:7 (AMP)	Hebrews 11:6 (ESV)	Jeremiah 1:12 (NKJV)

Paraphrased, Restated, or Summarized

Romans 6:23	John 1:1-14	Hebrews 10:22

Mentioned

Romans 5:12, 14	Hebrews 7:19	Hebrews 11:6
Exodus 26	Hebrews 7:25	
Hebrews 9	Hebrews 10:1	
Hebrews 4:16	Hebrews 10:22	

Chapter 3: The Preeminence of Christ in Prayer

Quoted

Colossians 1:15-20 (ESV)	Matthew 16:15 (ESV)	Psalm 82:1 (ESV)
John 1:15, 14 (ESV)	Matthew 16:16-17 (ESV)	Zechariah 3:1-2
Hebrews 11:3 (ESV)	Matthew 4:17 (ESV)	Revelation 12:10 (ESV)
Psalm 119:89 (ESV)	Matthew 16:18-19 (ESV)	1 John 2:1 (ESV)
Hebrews 7:22-25 (ESV)	John 4:4 (ESV)	Matthew 24:14 (ESV)
Colossians 1:18 (ESV)	John 12:32 (KJV)	
Luke 22:31-32 (ESV)	Colossians 1:19 (ESV)	

Paraphrased, Restated, or Summarized

Hebrews 11:3	John 10:10	Zechariah 3:3-5
2 Corinthians 3	Isaiah 9:6	

Mentioned

Genesis 1	Daniel 7:9-10	Matthew 16:18-19
1 Corinthians 2:7-12	Revelations 4:4	Matthew 4:8-9
Hebrews 7	Job 1:6	Matthew 12:26
Isaiah 53:3	Hebrews 12:1	2 Corinthians 4:4
1 Corinthians 2	Zechariah 3:1	Matthew 24
Psalm 89:7	1 Kings 22:19-23	
Jeremiah 23:18	Hebrews 6:20	

Chapter 4: Yoked with Christ

Quoted

Matthew 11:25-30 (ESV)	John 14:6-9 (ESV)	Hebrews 4:1-3 (ESV)
Matthew 13:10-13 (ESV)	Acts 3:19-20 (ESV)	2 Corinthians 3:18 (ESV)

Paraphrased, Restated, or Summarized

John 17:11

Mentioned

Hebrews 7:25	Matthew 10:1
Colossians 1:19	

Chapter 5: Intimacy with the Holy Spirit

Quoted

John 14:15-17 (ESV)	Acts 4:31 (ESV)	Romans 8:5-6 (ESV)
John 14:26 (ESV)	Acts 6:10 (ESV)	1 Corinthians 2:9-11
John 16:7-8, 13-15 (ESV)	Acts 10:44 (ESV)	(ESV)
Matthew 12:28 (ESV)	Acts 13:2 (ESV)	Romans 8:14-17 (ESV)
2 Corinthians 13:14	Acts 19:11-12 (ESV)	Romans 8:26-27 (ESV)
(ESV)	2 Corinthians 13:14	
Acts 1:8 (ESV)	(ESV)	

Paraphrased, Restated, or Summarized

Acts 5:12-16	John 10:10

Mentioned

Hebrews 3:7	Matthew 10:20	John 16:7
1 Timothy 4:1	Philippians 1:19	John 16:8-11
Romans 8:27	Acts 1:8	Matthew 12:28
Romans 15:30	Romans 12:3-8	1 Corinthians 12:3
1 Corinthians 12:11	1 Corinthians 12:1-13	Acts 2:38-39
Genesis 1:2	John 14:15-17	John 16:7-8, 13-15

Chapter 6: Partnership with the Holy Spirit

Quoted

2 Corinthians 3:7-8 (ESV)	2 Corinthians 3:16-18 (ESV)	Jeremiah 33:3 (ESV)
1 Corinthians 12:3 (ESV)	Matthew 6:6 (ESV)	Galatians 5:16 (ESV)
Titus 3:4-7 (ESV)	Romans 8:26 (ESV)	Galatians 5:25 (ESV)
2 Corinthians 5:17-21 (ESV)	Isaiah 11:2 (ESV)	Isaiah 30:15 (ESV)
	Matthew 26:41 (ESV)	Psalms 23:2-3 (ESV)
	Psalm 100:4 (ESV)	John 4:13-14 (ESV)
		John 7:37-39 (ESV)

Paraphrased, Restated, or Summarized

Acts 16:25-26

Mentioned

Hebrews 4:16

Interlude: With All Prayer

Quoted

Ephesian 6:18 (ESV)

Chapter 7: Intercessory Prayer

Quoted

2 Corinthians 5:18-21 (ESV)	Matthew 11:28 (ESV)	Jeremiah 23:9 (ESV)
Ephesians 2:4-7 (ESV)	Ephesians 6:18 (ESV)	1 Corinthians 14:2, 13-15 (ESV)
Mark 16:15-18 (ESV)	1 John 4:20-21 (ESV)	1 Corinthians 14:18 (ESV)
Matthew 28:18-20 (ESV)	Matthew 9:35-38 (ESV)	1 Corinthians 12:1, 4-6 (ESV)
Jeremiah 23:9 (ESV)	Isaiah 66:8 (ESV)	
Jeremiah 20:9 (ESV)	Isaiah 53:11 (KJV)	
	John 3:16-17 (ESV)	

Paraphrased, Restated, or Summarized

Ephesians 2:7	1 Corinthians 14:15

Mentioned

1 Corinthians 14:2	1 Corinthians 14:4-5	1 Corinthians 14:13

Chapter 8: Corporate Intercession

Quoted

Joel 1:14 (ESV)	Matthew 18:18 (ESV)	1 Corinthians 14:26-33 (ESV)
Psalm 50:5-6 (ESV)	Isaiah 66:8 (ESV)	Psalms 133:1-3 (ESV)
Matthew 18:20 (ESV)	Romans 12:3-8 (ESV)	Ephesians 4:11-14 (ESV)
Deuteronomy 4:9-13 (ESV)	1 Corinthians 12:4-11 (ESV)	

Paraphrased, Restated, or Summarized

Acts 2:41

Chapter 9: Prayer and...

Quoted

Matthew 6:16 (ESV)	John 4:23-24 (ESV)	1 Corinthians 14:24-25 (ESV)
Matthew 6:17-18 (ESV)	Amos 9:11 (ESV)	Revelation 19:10 (ESV)
Matthew 4:4 (ESV)	Acts 15:14-18 (ESV)	Peter 1:19-21 (ESV)
Matthew 5:6 (ESV)	Hebrews 13:15-16 (ESV)	Proverbs 18:14 (ESV)
Isaiah 58:3 (ESV)	1 Peter 2:5, 9-10 (ESV)	Psalm 19:7-9 (ESV)
Romans 8:5 (ESV)	Romans 12:1-2 (ESV)	Joel 2:28-29 (ESV)
Isaiah 58:4 (ESV)	Isaiah 30:10-11 (ESV)	Acts 2:16-18 (ESV)
Isaiah 58:6-9 (ESV)	Jonah 3:4 (ESV)	Romans 8:19 (ESV)
Galatians 5:1 (ESV)	Jonah 3:5 (ESV)	Acts 4:29-30 (ESV)
Matthew 17:21 (NKJV)	1 Corinthians 14:1, 3-5 (ESV)	Ephesians 1:17-23 (ESV)
Psalm 23:3 (ESV)		
Exodus 34:14 (ESV)		

Paraphrased, Restated, or Summarized

Matthew 6:17-18

Mentioned

Psalm 22:3	Psalm 100:4

Chapter 10: Releasing the Power of God

Quoted

Luke 5:15-17 (ESV)	Matthew 12:22 (ESV)	Acts 2:2-4 (ESV)
Luke 11:1 (ESV)	Matthew 7:21-23 (ESV)	John 10:30, 37-38 (ESV)
John 5:19-21 (ESV)	Acts 19:13-17 (ESV)	Romans 8:14-17 (ESV)
Acts 2:42-43 (ESV)	Luke 2:52 (ESV)	John 14:12 (ESV)
Matthew 12:25-28 (ESV)	Acts 1:8 (ESV)	

Paraphrased, Restated, or Summarized

John 11:1-44

Chapter 11: Spiritual Warfare

Quoted

Ephesians 2:2 (NKJV)	1 Corinthians 13:1-8 (ESV)	Isaiah 11:2-3 (ESV)
2 Corinthians 4:4 (NKJV)		John 8:44 (ESV)
Matthew 16:18-19 (ESV)	1 John 4:7-8 (ESV)	2 Corinthians 4:4 (ESV)
Hebrews 1:14 (ESV)	Exodus 20:18, 20 (ESV)	John 14:15 (ESV)
Joshua 5:13-14 (ESV)	1 Corinthians 3:10-15 (ESV)	Joel 2:12-14 (ESV)
Ephesians 6:13-18 (ESV)		Numbers 13:30 (ESV)
James 1:2-4 (ESV)	Proverbs 29:27 (ESV)	1 John 4:2-4 (ESV)

Paraphrased, Restated, or Summarized

Daniel 10	Galatians 5:22
1 Kings 22:19-23	Matthew 25:1-12

Mentioned

Ephesians 6:12	Daniel 10:20	Ephesians 3:10
Daniel 10:13	Ephesians 2:2	

Epilogue: Farewell Blessings

Quoted

Ephesians 1:17-23 (ESV)	Colossians 1:9-14 (ESV)	2 Thessalonians 1:11-12 (ESV)
Philippians 1:9-11 (ESV)	Romans 15:5-7, 13 (ESV)	

www.ingramcontent.com/pod-product-compliance
Lightning Source LLC
Chambersburg PA
CBHW080225140626
46555CB00020B/3018